C00 45694915

Th  EDINBURGH

D1766092

Love

⌐44
3J
506
.D4

c
t

Peter G Mackie

Published by
Chipmunkapublishing
PO Box 6872
Brentwood
Essex CM13 1ZT
United Kingdom

http://www.chipmunkapublishing.com

Copyright © Peter Mackie 2010

Edited by Regine Pilling

Chipmunkapublishing gratefully acknowledge the support of Arts Council England.

Author Biography

Peter G Mackie was born in Perth, Scotland in 1957 and, as a teenager, was mistakenly kept in an Adolescent Unit of a psychiatric hospital for two and a half years, an experience which affected his whole life and which led him to suffer from depression.

Due to problems with his family, he ran away from home at the age of 16 and suffered abuse on the streets of London.

At the age of 17, after a brief period in a hippy commune, he wrote his novel The Madhouse of Love in a bed-sit in Tooting, South London, based on his earlier experiences in the psychiatric unit.

From 1977 to 1984, he spent a period working and travelling in Europe, which helped him to see a different perspective on life.

However, due to unemployment in the 1980s, he was forced to return to Scotland, where he took an HND in Computer Data Processing, but failed to find work in that field.

Due to his education having been disrupted early in life, he has had to survive doing unskilled jobs interspersed with periods of unemployment.

From 2001 to 2007, he went through a very difficult time, moving from place to place, trying to find work and accommodation, with little success, causing him to have a nervous breakdown and to lapse again into depression.

He ended up homeless in Edinburgh, where he sold The Big Issue for over a year.

He is now doing an IT course at Redhall Walled Garden, a project in Edinburgh run by the Scottish Association for Mental Health (SAMH) and is still struggling hard to cope with depression.

During the 1980s and '90s, he had poems published in numerous small press magazines.

He has also recorded a CD of music on piano and synthesiser All Over the Shop, which is available from some alternative shops in Edinburgh and over the Internet.

Due to his experiences both earlier and later in life, he has a particular concern for the rights of young people, for those claiming disability benefits and for the homeless.

Chapter 1

It was the spring of 1969.

I had been acting the goat.

My mother said, "There must be something far wrong with him."

So they called in the psychiatrist from the local lunatic asylum. He said, "There is nothing wrong with that boy. He is merely acting the goat."

After the doctor had left, my father shouted at me, with threats to send me to Borstal, since it was only on the grounds of illness that he would tolerate such behaviour.

On holiday that summer, in the north of Scotland, while watching stock-car racing, nature called, so I said that I was going behind a bush.

When my father heard this, he threw me down on the ground and held me fast, almost crushing me.

I thought that he was going to kill me.

I screamed.

He told me to stop shouting and screaming like a madman, that there were people about who would call the police and have me put in prison.

My brother Hamish begged him to leave me alone and took us back to our uncle's house in the car. I lay in the back seat, tears streaming down my face.

It was the 17th of August 1969, one month after the Moon landings and on the third day of Woodstock festival.

I was going to this place to see a doctor who was going to use me as a guinea pig.

I thought that it might be a bit of a laugh. So, during the interview, I acted the goat.

I was to be an in-patient, starting that day, and would probably only be there for a few days. They took me along to the dormitory.

I was brought in howling and screaming. I was told, "You are now going to meet someone who will be a great friend – George".

The remedy considered, 50 m.g. Largactil by mouth, I took willingly as an alternative to the rumoured intromuscular injection. As I tried to keep calm, my lying prostrated in silence for a few seconds was met by, from the gruff voice of the male nurse:

"Is this sleep, or is it hysterical death?"

There was a knock at the door.

"Come in. It's all right."

A suntanned girl of 14 entered, asking:

"Is this the new laddie?"

She was answered by Lorna, the ugly nurse, who nodded:

"Are you going to the canteen?"

I imagined the canteen as a cross between a restaurant and a school canteen.

"What's your name?"

"Ann."

"Ann who?"

"Ann Zubrowka."

"And what's your name?"

"Tony."

"I've been hearing you play the piano."

Ann organised us all to go out for a walk. On the way down the road, she talked about her ex-boyfriends and how she couldn't see the modern sculptures at the Camperdown Park, Dundee, because of this daft boy. She'd apparently been at art college there. We went past the swings and ate some sweets. It was a beautiful summer's day.

I, Tony, the 12-year-old phenomenon would often sit on a bench in one of the two sitting rooms during the summer's days, looking towards my distant future which lay away in the parts of the sky which shone yellow with the sun and at which I would arrive if I could only manage to discharge myself.

It was on one fine summer's night that a pale figure – a mirror image of myself – was seen wandering around the hospital unit. This was that other phenomenon, 13-

year-old Dave Chambers, who questioned all the boys: "Are you interested in homosexuality?" and would keep informing everyone: "I don't like poofs." That same Dave Chambers, on the beautiful night of his arrival, whispered, "I like Tony," on seeing myself, and talked about how he liked to express his feelings in painting.

In the mornings, there was the assembly: this consisted of a group discussion where everyone said what he or she felt or didn't say what he or she didn't feel. At this particular time, it was fairly intellectual and Dr. Martin, the psychiatrist, was able to preach his religion about it. Every morning, Duncan with the red hair played the signature tune of *Dr. Kildare* to Dr. Martin, while I would sit at the front hall, waiting for him, looking at the cars flashing their lights of Freud, God, sex and insanity through the hospital grounds.

Then, the old character himself would walk in with his hat and wide-lapelled suit.

The conversations would be something like this:

"I'd like to complain about the baking rota."

"You want to complain about the baking rota? But that's the feminine arts, isn't it?"

"But not all girls like baking, Dr. Martin!"

"Do many of you feel disappointed with your sex?"

"What a funny question, Dr. Martin!"

Of course, at nights were the real times. Dave would sit on his bed, saying that interplanetary space travel would be common in twenty years' time while Alan Oldham, the night charge, would tell him that he was talking nonsense.

Dave was one for watching science fiction programmes on the television. There was one particular one about ESP.

I would often have appointments with Dr. Martin at 9 o'clock in the morning. There was one night, before my appointment, when I was talking to Mary Parsons, one of the girls, about it and whether I was insane or not. She said, "Of course, you're not insane!" Boo hoo, it makes me want to sob to think of it. And Duncan would have to come in and play *Dr. Kildare* in the middle of it. Plink, plonk.

One night, I grew very frightened of the idea of beards. I began thinking of ways in which they could be cut, e.g. grown into two very long points and cut very short in the centre. The idea disgusted me so much that I was physically sick in the sink.

Often, I would play around with the skin on the end of my nose and chin, which somehow had a feeling of awkwardness about it, so often described as "perverse pleasure". In fact, once, in school, I had nipped my finger in the desk and closed the lid hard on the nipped part, so that it stood on end for about a minute after I had taken it out.

I also had my times of dreaming thoughts going through my mind. One of these times, I became certain that a boy I knew quite well was a direct descendant of Macbeth.

At night, in bed, Dave used to talk for ages about Einstein, or some other scientific subject, or else something from his life, such as the time he took an overdose, or the time he was raped by homosexuals, or the time he received a shock from a van der Graaf generator, or the boy in his class at school who had a completely bald head. On his wall, he had stuck some strange pictures out of magazines. One of them was supposed to represent people being driven insane by the full moon.

The other two who slept in the dormitory were Duncan, with the red hair, and little Johnny Smith. One night, I was lying quietly in bed and these three had been talking for some time, when they somehow got it into their heads to haul me out of bed. They pulled the covers and the mattress off, while I was still lying on it, not paying any attention.

When it came near to Christmas, I had an advent calendar. Every day, they tore more and more of it apart until, about two weeks before Christmas, there was nothing left of it.

Occupying a room at the top end of the corridor, next to the staff office, was Vincent. I had heard about him the first day I arrived. I was told that he was a good chess player.

I remember the night I gave him his first game of chess.

That was the one and only time that I beat him. In between moves, I looked around with interest at his hamster running around and at the flies moving around the room. Vincent had a great interest in animals and in nature.

The Madhouse of Love

Two rooms down from Vincent lived Jim McCann. He was below normal intelligence and did everything his parents wanted him to do.

In the bottom room lived Dave and the other two rooms were empty.

When I arrived, there were only three girls.

Mary Parsons was the best loved. She had gone with more of the boys than either of the other two. She went with Dave for a long time, and he went around wearing her skirt once of twice.

Jane Thornton was an asthmatic and she kept getting discharged and readmitted for this reason.

Mary Martin was the most beautiful as far as I was concerned. She, however, fancied herself as a boy.

I was asked what I wanted for breakfast. I asked for cornflakes and an egg roll.

I sat eating the cornflakes, my mind drifting in sadness and weeping silently. Ann watched me and laughed at me, and had a communication with me about it.

I lay in bed, looking at the two lights.

The doors were open. I could walk out of there any time, apparently. But I couldn't, or they would put me in an approved school or somewhere.

I knocked the girls' Tampax out of their drawers, such as when about a dozen of us were sitting in Mary Parsons' room with the door closed.

I sat with them in the school at night, with slanting roof and huge round lamps, watching television programmes about hysteria and sexy love affairs.

I would stare out the window at the hills in the afternoon or at nights.

School hadn't started and Johnny Nero, our new teacher, hadn't arrived.

Dave and I had some union, as we both met each other and understood each other more than other people we met.

I sat at the piano playing out of a book waltzes or other music such as Mozart's *Rondo.*

As I sat in the sitting room with or without others, I contemplated the view and the grain of the wood on the shelf. The picture of a sea full of ships in the staff office had something to do with my trying to get out of the place somehow.

I went down to try to see Dr. Martin one Saturday morning to say that I was only putting on an act and wasn't really ill, but I couldn't bring myself around to do so.

Ann and Martime, the other temporary nurse who was with her, took us for a cycling trip. We pedalled about five miles to a nearby village and parked at the village green by the inn. We sat in the lounge.

Ann became all worked up and said, "Tony's parents might be Methodist or something, and wouldn't like him to be on premises selling alcohol;" then, turning to me after talking about me behind my back, asked, "Do your parents sometimes go out for a drink?"

"Yes."

Barry Wagstaff, an orphan, went through the bar to go to the toilet. On coming back, he told us, "That bar's full of dirty men! One of them told me to wank off!"

On the way back, I saw various walls and landmarks, and actually thought that a car driving past was my parents' car and stopped Ann, and the rest of them must have wondered what I was doing.

On the Wednesday after I was admitted, my parents had visited and we sat in the Visitors' Room which had, on the walls, prints of a nude by Picasso and van Gogh's *The Sower* and my mother cried.

After that, they came every weekend and took me out for runs in the car. I would come back from them and have a slice of toast, while two girl nurses from the Children's Unit were having their tea.

We all stood by the roundel, when we had nothing to do or didn't want to be on our own. I stood with them who said, "I'm fed up." And would bash a bag of rubbish against the wall several times, shouting, "A wee whilie", while Gregg made faces and shouted, "Glonk, glonk!"

The roundel, incidentally, was a round passage in the centre of which were the boys' and girls' locker rooms.

I had been a patient twice before. Once, at the age of ten, in a general hospital where the boys were at one side of the ward and the girls at the other side, and an oxygen cylinder was brought in one night in an emergency for one girl. I did something I shouldn't have one night and was taken by a nurse to a small room, was given a ticking off and read the Dandy.

I stared at the windows at nights and planned to run out the Fire Escape.

I was in there for brain tests.

A year later, I was in another hospital, not so general this time, which was a bore. We wandered around on the green grass and sang songs on the mini-bus on the way back from the swimming baths.

The only happy moment was when they took a picture of me with my arm around a girl. Her name was Heather White and the only thing to say about her is that, one night, she was taken to appear in a fashion parade.

We climbed up the climbing bars. When we went to the gym on a Tuesday morning, I looked up at the huge lampshade made of mirrors, which reflected in different colours and, when lying face down, I spread out my arms and imagined I was an aeroplane.

We all walked up to the snack bar every Tuesday afternoon to buy sweets, and I was visited by my parents, who took me out for a walk every Wednesday evening.

And there was the free expression room with its walls covered with paint.

We went to see the crafts teacher at 9 o'clock in the morning, which I liked, or at least liked better than the rest of the time.

The Madhouse of Love

And now I was in for the third time.

I remember when I first got home for a weekend and the thrill I got when I first told Marie Davidson about it. I sat with my parents in a restaurant. In the village square that night, some rowdy boys were shouting and singing:

"Dinah, Dinah, show us a leg
 A yard above the knee!"

Out the back window was a load of rubbish: bricks, weeds, an empty packet of Dr. White's.

I went for a walk around the hospital every afternoon and, in the mornings, I would walk around the Unit and look in Dr. Martin's window to see if he was in.

Later, I would go on walks with others, such as one winter's night when I went for a walk with Viv and Marie down to the village. We walked back through the fields full of cows at the back of the police station, and I said, "If anyone saw us, they would think we were three cows!" Then we came on to the road lined with trees where cars flashed their headlamps and behind which lay the madhouse of love.

Over farther fields was the town where the girls and boys sat in cafes and bought clothes; and the road along which we talked about "White reminds me of madness". As I walked along the road, I heard the birds singing and the hooter hooting.

The Nurses' Home was full of temporary nurses. I could have conversations with Ann about the superficiality of the rest of the staff, who didn't think.

I could have conversations with Vincent, who took walks on his own as I did.

The low and high hills around made a deep impression on my mind.

There was a print of a Modigliani painting in the corridor, which was known as "that Mogdileeny thing". One night, I said to Dave, "Picasso and Mogadon were talking together one night..."

Mogadon is a sleeping tablet.

Dave said, "I thought you were talking about the bloke that painted that Mogdileeny thing."

Janus Mitchell would say to me sadly, "There's a brilliant piece of music on the piano called *Largo*." I would play it and she would play it. Thump, thump, thump.

I would like in bed naked and get raped.

We would sit in the front hall when we had nothing to do.

As for this romantic business about the mind, I imagined the mind as a piece of flint stone, with different layers: conscious, subconscious, unconscious.

I danced with girls in the dark, thought of flying to galaxies. That Sunday night, little Johnny came back from his weekend at home in a red poloneck sweater and I thought, "Some nice girl'll fancy him."

Down the corridor I shouted and went with my life in my hands and, in the mornings, I opened the curtains to admire the beauties of nature and take a cold shower at 7 o'clock.

Dr. Martin had said to me that there was a sensible Tony and a silly Tony – in fact, two Tonies inside me. I pondered over this.

I often drew and wrote – even early in the mornings such things as would venture into my mind: for instance, a bearded man wearing a suit covered in question marks.

I started to half-believe what the staff were telling me, but I knew that not everything they said was true. They have an insidious way of trying to persuade one, which doesn't work with some creatures, who are "very clever" or "just like Male Ward 6".

My talks with the charge nurses were always in conflict, and one of them once remarked,
"Tony and I never did see eye to eye anyhow!"

And, one night, I sat thumping on the piano and worked myself into a state whereat I was considered to be completely out of my mind.

I was "abnormal" and "emotionally disturbed" and, therefore, not fit to live in the normal world with normal people.

This community, this institution, this group of committed individuals into which I was involuntarily forced was similar in a vague way to a therapeutic community which I was to attempt to join four years later. I was more in tune with the former, however.

When, three years later, one afternoon by the sea, I felt that I had to speak to them and see the place again, I made an appointment with Dr. Martin for the following Saturday. On the way home, I read Vincent's poetry. He had just come back from London and had been readmitted as a result of a row with his parents.

I remember the impetus of the poems against the background of black night, sitting in the bus station café eating doughnuts.

Well, the days went by – fortunately more slowly at that time.

I spent a great deal of time in my room, where I would sit reading, thinking or looking out the window at the world of trees, wind, occasional people and cars in the distance going by. Or I would go for walks around the hospital.

How can I tell you the ecstasy and the agony of having breakfast, going to school, the gym, table tennis, the doctors, everything?

I will go on.

On about love, life and dreams.

I would wander calmly and restlessly through my piano mind, and, at nights, in a rage, I would scribble and write the awfullest rubbish on to paper.

Serenely and delicately, I would travel through aeons of my own thought and masturbate in galaxies of sanity.

The Madhouse of Love

Truth blended in front of my eyeballs. On the toilet, I would silently meditate and see the pattern of life staring me in the face of the tiled floor.

Then someone would shout, "Last call for tea!" and I would pile the marmalade on to doorsteps of bread.

The teacher would play classical music in the school, which I would feel that I was eating.

The sound of my music and the sight of my mind would please many people: doctors, nurses, patients, social workers, students, people's parents, anyone who happened to wander in. I was the life and soul of the place, the personality, the character of the Unit.

I was famous in my own way then. I was the idol of hundreds of people, with whom I would come into contact.

My dreams would be something like crawling through a tunnel, trying to but failing to come out into the open, where there were green fields and people playing sports.

In fact, that is what I have always been doing every since. Crawling through a tunnel, trying to but failing to come out into the open where there are green fields and people playing sports.

I was pushed out of normal life and thrown into a black, claustrophobic dungeon. Where I would only sit and wonder.

Everywhere around me from the hospital farm to the admission ward will always permeate my mind.

Shadowy, dreamily, they travel around it like a satellite orbiting some long lost planet light years away.

Graciously and paranoically over my psyche spat visions of boys and girls looking as if they were ready to go to bed.

These were the times, though. I could easily imagine myself making love to someone, I could easily imagine poetry. I could easily imagine everything that mattered.

We sat in the school listening to music and lightning flashed behind the hills.

Dr. Martin said that Dave and I would be staying there all winter. I thought, "Oh God! I won't be able to stand it that long!"

One night, in the four-bedder, Duncan looked across to my bed and remarked, "He's tossin' off!"

The conversation had been going like this:

"Mind you, it is good to be at a Celtic and Rangers match!"

"What's that got to do with why a woman's tits stick up?"

Of course, I didn't know what I was doing and naturally thought that I was doing something strange and abnormal.

Another night, I shouted out, "Quiblic, quiblic, 1.2.3." and climbed out of bed naked to go to the toilet. The nurse told me to go back to bed.

The Madhouse of Love

I will always remember Ann Zubrowka. She was half-Irish, half-Polish. She gave me a poster she had drawn of a boy in her class at art college and I hung it on my wall upside-down. A temporary nurse, having worked for two weeks with another of the same, she decided to stay on and did so until March, having started in August.

One night, her boy-friend, who was later to become her husband, came to see us in a converted Post Office van. He was introduced to me. Ann had told him that I wrote poetry, so I gave him a copy of one. After he left, he said to Ann, "Was he supposed to be daft? He didn't look daft." The next week, he came back and asked me if I could write some children's stories for a comic, for which he did a page every week. I tried, but, apparently, my efforts were of no use.

Ann went about the hospital with Nurse Andrews, a Dutch nurse, who was always making Bircher-Benner health foods and organised parties every second Sunday night.

There was a tree, which I always associated with Ann, at the bottom of the lawn behind the hospital unit. I thought that it was very graceful, despite the fact that it never grew any leaves. I told my teacher that it was a carnivorous tree, but the word was, of course, "coniferous".

During assembly one morning, Ann was chewing gum, when one of the boys asked her, "What are you chewing?", to which she replied, sarcastically, "I don't really know. I found it on the floor." Dr. Martin kept picking fluff from his jacket when people were speaking to him. His jacket was also crumpled. He asked me what I was laughing at. Of course, that was what it was.

Very often, some of us would go into the school at night to paint. Ann often came, and painted well. I remember getting really excited with my paintings: they were mostly quiet landscapes, one of which was covered with a huge black tree.

It was a great characteristic of Ann and I to go out the back door and jump around like mad and shout wonderful things. I often wish nowadays that I was back in these times.

There were silent times when I always wanted to be on my own. During one such mood, I walked down the corridor, shouting, "Oooooh-oooh", when Vincent came out of his room and asked if I was all right. "I was just having a carry on," I replied.

During other quiet periods, I thought to myself about such things as paintings, poetry, astronomy, dreams etc. Some of these times, I thought of people being damned to Hell and tried to accommodate this idea in my mind. I had pictures of people's dreams, which had appeared in connection with an article in a magazine, on my wall, and so did Dave Chambers, who was in the room next to me. Bill Whittington, a male nurse, came in at a time like this and, after a short conversation, said, "Paintings and dreams are strange things. I don't pretend to understand them."

About 4 o'clock one afternoon, Dr. Martin summoned me for a talk. I followed him into the gymnasium. He asked me, "Do you think this is a big enough room for us?" He was explaining some sort of explosion of energy within the mind: "It suddenly goes POOF! – ah, poof is an unfortunate word –". Soon after this, I began to look away through the skylight. He told me that I kept looking away, it was a sign that I was going into a dream.

Martha, one of the nurses, presently set me in her wig. Ann helped. Dr. Martin said to me later, "It's dangerous, this business, you know, wearing wigs and things. It makes you think that you're another person."

One time, when I was lying on the dining room floor, Ann looked at me and said that I looked like a girl. I liked that, for some reason.

Ann and I spent most of the time discussing the paintings hanging in the building, and music.

One day, in the early spring, a party of us took a walking trip to the cattle market in the village about two miles away. Ann sat with her finger poised on her lips, staring into space. She was getting married in two weeks' time. She had told me a few days before, when I was sticking pictures on my wall with Plasti-Tak.

When I asked Dr. Martin when she was leaving, he didn't even know about it.

Dr. Martin was forever pestering me with questions. One evening, he asked me, "If your parents, for some reason, couldn't come to collect you to take you home for the weekend, and you wanted to go home, how would you go?" He seemed to think that I wouldn't know. I only wished that I could have a chance to go home by myself, so I could have some freedom to do what I wanted for once, without people bothering me about every little thing I did.

In his room were various books. One was called something like *The Psychology of the Abnormal Person*. There were also *Memories, Dreams, Reflections* and *Man and His Symbols* by Carl G. Jung, the latter of which he had received as a present from one of his patients, who was a doctor. On the mantelpiece was a purple glass paperweight, which he later took away to his flat in the hospital. Below the mantelpiece was the chair in which he sat talking to his patients and smoking his pipe.

He would talk about the awakening of the sexual instincts during puberty, and maintain that, during the so-called "latency" period, they lay "dormant, latent, quiescent". There was something about the way in which he drawled the words "dormant, latent, quiescent" which seemed almost hypnotic and made a strange echo through my mind.

One night, Dave and I were sitting in the dormitory, when the former said to me, "Dr. Martin's supposed to be coming round tonight." I waited in anticipation. After talking about space travel and astronomy over Dave's books for a while, he eventually did come round. He started explaining about the conscious and the unconscious mind. Dave asked him, "Which is the better, the conscious or unconscious?" to which Dr. Martin replied, "Well, let's put it this way, the unconscious is the more natural and, if it's ignored, you're in trouble."

Next morning, after the assembly, I played the piano, which I did at that time every morning. Dr. Martin said that I was a good pianist. The subject that morning was homosexuality. Gregg, a boy who screamed and shouted when annoyed, never washed himself and ran around shouting, "Schwein Hund", asked in a loud voice to Dr. Martin, "Did you know that Oscar Wilde was a poof?", to which the latter replied, "Everyone knows that."

School had started by this time. The teacher, who was bald, wore a beard and a kilt, after having given us an English lesson with homework to compare Coleridge's *The Rime of the Ancient Mariner* with Lewis Carroll's *The Hunting of the Snark*, let us each pick a library book. I chose one about a little boy living in the Arctic, to the north of Norway, in the winter. Inside the front cover, I kept a sheet where I marked the number of weeks I thought I would have to stay in the hospital, and ticked one off every week. (In actual fact, my total stay amounted to two and a half years). The next book I took out was a book about astronomy called *Kingdom of the Sun*. It contained information about the history of the theories of many astronomers, particularly Ptolemy and Copernicus – also included were Kepler and Tycho Brahe – and I was really in an ecstasy reading it. Every night, I sat in the sitting room to read it, looking out the window to the starry sky, which was getting dark earlier by this time. After I had read till 8 o'clock, I would go out the front door, walk around the hospital unit once, and sit for around ten minutes looking at the starry sky.

Very often, in the evenings, a lot of us would take out the wallbars and ropes in the gymnasium. One night, when I was swinging on a rope, Dave asked me, "Is the thing between your legs hurting you?" Then, some of us went over to play the piano for a while. I played the *Rondo* by Mozart a lot, which they all liked.

A few weeks after I had been admitted, two girls, Marie Davidson and Janus Mitchell were also admitted, the latter of whom word got round had spent a night in prison. It was thought terrible. Marie said that she was in because she had been raped. They were not allowed to go out for walks together. If they both went out at the same time, it was observed that they went in different directions. Before this arrangement had been made, however, I went out with them both together one night. We walked up to the bus shelter. Marie was smoking a cigarette. She asked me if I wanted a draw. I had never smoked. I said, "Yes." I coughed and spluttered on it.

On the way back, we met a girl whom Marie had known, who had run away from home. When we got back, I was told off by the staff for "getting involved".

One morning, Dr. Martin and I were talking alone in the dormitory. He mentioned to me that, in psychoanalysis, he was looking for one thought which was not a conscious thought, and which lay behind all my actions. I asked him if that thought would be subconscious or completely unconscious. He replied, "I'm very sorry, my mind was wandering."

Hanging around the school one day, talking to the teacher, was a tall boy with long, dark hair. I wondered who this could be. It did not strike me that he was a new patient; in fact, at one point, I thought that he might have been the new teacher of whom it had been spoken that we were to have.

Later on, however, he was introduced to me. This was Billy Mason. The next day, I was wandering around behind the Adolescent Unit, as the place was called, and the Children's Unit, which lay next to it, walked round the front, came in and played the piano and he shouted, "Mozart".

The Madhouse of Love

His sister, Vivien, was admitted as an out-patient later in the week. She used to hang around the school and paint with this next character I will describe.

Billy Ronson. He was a kleptomaniac, we were told. "He'll steal funny things from you, like knickers." Very intelligent was he, and he painted well.

One afternoon, when we were both sitting around the piano, he most beautifully and passionately played Beethoven's *Für Elise*. I felt that I was soaring in an ecstasy like a bird into the sky.

Around that weekend came the next admission. Gregg Anderson. He talked in a strange voice and tended to shout. At his coming-in party, he, Billy Ronson, Dave and I talked about astronomy and scientific things generally.

That night in the four-bedder (as the dormitory was called), we did exercises. Next morning, when Billy Ronson, who was an out-patient, arrived in, he boasted having done twenty press-ups as soon as he had risen out of bed.

Very soon after these admissions came two girls, both of whom had obsessions with keeping their weight down. They were Lorna Morrison and Lorna Duncan.

Lorna Morrison had spent some years in America and still had a slight American accent. She always took "Saxin" pills in her tea instead of sugar.

Lorna Duncan was very tall, had long hair and was very quiet. The day she came in, Ann drew her portrait, which she hung on her bedroom wall.

It was November. We heard that we were going to have a new teacher and had seen people wandering around applying for the job.

It was morning. I had just finished breakfast and remember coming out of the toilet to see a dark-haired, bearded character walk past me. He turned around, noticed me and stopped.

"Johnny Nero, your new teacher."

"Tony."

When assembly was over, we got into school and he took us for class. He stood majestically in front of us and started bawling in a broad Aberdonian accent to tell us that, in their council house in Aberdeen, they had taken the door off their bedroom and all the locks off all the doors in the house, replacing them with an Alsatian guard dog. Other things which were his boast were the following: he and his wife had been arrested for keeping chickens illegally in their garden, which could not be seen from any other house, road or human thoroughfare; they had been struck off the medical list because he had, at the birth of one of their children, asked the midwife how many children she had, to which she replied that she was not married, at which Johnny made it clear that he had not asked her whether or not she was married; they had been illegally put out of their house and were taken in by two students, one of whom was a drug-addict and later became an alcoholic and moved to the Orkney Islands, and the other of whom played the violin; when Johnny had once worked as a bus conductor, he had not charged any of the passengers; when he was a student, being compelled to attend a dinner at which he had to be dressed in a collar and tie and his undergraduate's gown, he turned up wearing all these, underneath which he wore no shirt and a pair of swimming trunks.

It was over a year after his arrival, when I was on the chore of washing the dishes, that I discovered that the mini-bus which took us to the swimming baths every Thursday had left and realised, consequently, that I would have to join the non-swimmers in the school with Johnny.

When we got into the school, he produced a book which he had taken out of the library, entitled *The Other Love*, from which he lectured us on Sodom and Gomorrah, Oscar Wilde, W. Somerset Maugham and the author of the Eton boating song plus many more. Before we left, he asked us to whom we thought the writer had dedicated the book. It was his wife.

Johnny had a good sense of humour. Once, when we were editing the school magazine, he had made up a question and answer game. One of the questions was regarding national costume; we had to pick the odd one out. He said that the odd one out was the kimono because "a man cannot wear a kimono". One of the boys then asked him, "Have you not seen Tony wearing his kimono?", to which he replied, "No, I must admit that he always takes it off before we go to bed."

When I described him to Ann, she said that she thought that he was daft.

I think that I am right in saying that it was the night of the 14th of December that I had a vivid dream, which I will always remember and which I shall now describe:
A girl was wandering around nude from the waist downwards. Then the dream seemed to become all

dark blue, about ultramarine shade. I was then in the back of a car, and my brother and a girl were having sex in the front, and somehow I seemed to be in the place of my brother at the same time. Then, somehow, Bill Whittington, the charge nurse, seemed to be driving the car and he turned into a policeman.

For a while after this, there were patterns of Aurora Borealis in a background of black sky, similar to pictures I had recently seen in astronomy books.

Then, the dream turned bright red and there was a room which was, in some way, akin to the O.T. room in the hospital, but was in another building.

Then the dream changed again and I was standing outside with Mary Thomson, one of the girls in the Unit. I was somehow very depressed. We saw a very ordinary-looking car start up. Mary said, "It's a monkey Victor!" At this point, the car became much bigger and black, as if it was a Rolls Royce transporting some important person, such as the Prime Minister, after which it drew past a large, yellow building, filling the whole picture of the dream, and across the side of the car was painted a huge rainbow.

During this period of my life, I also had many other very vivid and colourful dreams, the most lurid of which was the following dream which I had had the previous summer:

Two old men were standing at the side of the road in a small country town, while two horse-drawn carts passed by. One of the old men said to the other, "What number are these?" (meaning registration number, as in a car). At this point, a voice said loudly, "Maybe they knew more about horses and carts in the days of horses and carts than they know now."

After this, the dream became a black void, across which flashed bright colours, while a voice thundered, "The dawning of a new age".

This made a profound impression of me at the time.

Eventually Christmas came round. It was during the period up to the Christmas holidays that I started writing poetry, the very first example of which was as follows:

THE BLACK TREE PATTERN

In winter time,
          the black-looking trees
                    make special patterns
Which will register
          in your mind
                    and will stay there

               Until one day
               When you'll get away
               From these trees
               To a different breeze.

This new breeze
  Will take over
    Wholly
      From the old breeze
        And the memories
          Of old
            Will go deeper
            And deeper
            And you will
              Be living
              In a different world
              Altogether.
                Sometimes
                  You'll look back
                  And see
                    These old memories
                    And think
                      You were much happier
                      But if you are
                      Wise enough
                      You will not
                        Believe it.

The Madhouse of Love

Because
    The good matters
        More than the bad
            So you remember
                The good far more.
                And this is
                    All part
                        Of time's
                            Great illusions.
                                There are illusions
                                Of time
                                    As well as
                                        Of space
                                            And the illusions
                                            Of space
                                                Are optical.

I went home for the Christmas holidays. I remember sitting in the drawing room, looking out the window, trying to draw the general scene: the garden, the stream, the railway, the worksheds, the church, the hillslopes. Little do I remember of Christmas Day.

For New Year, I was brought back to the Unit. Shortly after I arrived back, I admitted masturbating to Dr. Martin for the first time. He mentioned in conversation that God had said, "Thou shalt not masturbate." This worried me. I lay down on my bed for a long time thinking it over, wondering if I was going to be condemned to Hell. That night, when he came round, he said to me, "And you will have your own thoughts."

At this time, I was reading an abridged edition of *The Canterbury Tales*, which I had taken out of the library. In the book, there were illustrations which showed peculiarly beards and the hair on the chest. When the cleaning lady found me reading it, she said, "You ought to read some comics for a change, you toffee-nose."

I remember New Year's Eve. Some sort of drink had been made up. It was certainly not very intoxicating, whatever it was. Some of them went out in their dressing-gowns to celebrate, but I went to bed a few minutes after twelve had struck.

And that was the end of The Sixties.

Early in the New Year, I was moved into a single room. About this time, some student nurses came for shorter and longer periods from a fortnight to several months. They took us out for walks at night.

These walks would last about five miles. We often walked through the estate of some rich, probably titled people, which was nearby, and also through a disused priory. One night, during one of these walks, a boy called Willie Pope started talking to cows through a fence. One student nurse remarked that I was quite content to quietly appreciate nature, with which I agreed.

Another time, we walked by the side of the river till we came to a small town and back by the main road, and I held a girl's hand all the way. I will always remember the quiet peace of that evening.

The first student nurse to come was John Brunston. He had dark hair and wore a grey suit. It was his habit to compliment me on little things which I did, for example, drawings. He told me that one drawing which I had done looked like a trout's brain. He had done his bit of fishing. Once, in school, when we were all asked to write a poem, he, being present and taking part, wrote about a trout.

Two mornings after John had arrived, I spied a strange, dark, bearded character sitting at the desk of the staff office writing notes. This was Jim Donaldson, the second student nurse.

He was a much deeper personality than the first. He had spent two years in the Navy, and had tried his hand at painting. His wife and he had a dog and a bitch, which they would frequently bring to the Unit in their car.

Often he and Dave spent a long time talking deep thoughts in Dave's room. One night, he, Dave, myself and Vincent, who suffered very badly from nerves and stammered, got into a conversation about God. When Vincent said that he believed that God was everywhere, Jim stepped in by saying that he believed that the planets, stars and galaxies were electrons, atoms and cells in the body of God and that we human beings were all gods in the same fashion. According to his theory, the Earth was doomed, being part of an infected cell, and we may even be the infection in the cell.

As I have mentioned, he had tried his hand at painting. He told me of a still life he had done for someone, which consisted of objects on a table, including a Bible and a lamp. When he went to have it framed, he was offered £30 for it, which he declined, having promised it to someone.

By this time, spring was well on the way. I was writing more poetry than ever, with which the school magazine was filled. I kept all my poems on little pieces of paper in a folder, which was gradually becoming more and more torn.

More and more student nurses and social workers started coming in and wandering around. I shall start with the ones I remember most.

We were all sitting assembled for the assembly and had been kept waiting for a while when, at long last, Dr. Martin came in with a strange man. Introducing him: "This is Abdul." "WHAAT!?" blurted out Gregg. "Now, I'm not going to repeat it. When Gregg met that nun from the Children's Unit, he had the same reaction. Gregg dislikes everything except plain, ordinary Scottish."

Abdul was very interested in my music and very tolerant of "daft bastards", "poofs", "cretins", "people all mixed up whose minds are a load of blobs" etc., as was that nun from the Children's Unit.

This benefactor of mankind must have manifested her personage on the vicinity of the Adolescent Shithouse some very beautiful spring day, when birds were singing, similar to a day the next year when I remember seeing a beautiful girl, who must have belonged to one of the staff cottages, walk up the road past the hospital. The first memory I associate with her was one time when she was sitting on the sideboard in the kitchen with Dave and myself standing around, and we had a brilliant conversation about things we thought and felt, like poetry, like God, like mental hospitals, like.... And where has all this gone now? .... People have raped my life so much that it is much more difficult to feel such energy.

All sorts of spontaneous things happened that summer. One very hot day we had our meals outside. After tea, I ran after one of the boys with the milk jug and threw it towards him, smashing it, with milk running all over the place. My energetic feelings were so strong that, after this, I painted in the school, and the colours were aggressive acting out of emotion in bright scarlet, orange, yellow. When the aggression died down, the smaller details I painted became paler, milder and greyer like a lull after a storm.

Another warm night that summer, I was in my room reading a science fiction book. I heard the fire alarm going, but didn't pay much attention as I was so absorbed in my book. It kept ringing for ages. Still I kept on reading. When I came round for supper that night, I heard the full story. Two of the boys, Paul and Andy Jackson, had set fire to a load of hay in the hospital farm .... the farm that I was later to walk past with girls in spring .... life is such a mysterious thing .... Oh hell!

Hell just like the time I cried that summer I was taken in when people tried to talk to me and persuade me the truth and said how I was such a nice-looking laddie and I wanted to strip naked to them all.... Just like the time I was brought in looking very unsexual and I shouted, "Get that woman out of my sight" at Vivian of my life.... I wanted to dress in a school uniform to be like other kids in schools having girl-friends and not having my life raped............... I made love to everyone mentally at that time.... playing games of Monopoly.... ready to make love to any of them who wanted but none of them did or seemed to ..... trying to send music and poetry to publishers who didn't publish it, to love people with my music and poetry – posting the poetry and meeting one of the doctors who gave me a lift back – watching kids riding ponies on the road to town – the hills go up and down and my nature is up and down and ran away - I wanted do drown myself – I showed my brother love when he visited me.

What a wonderful world to be alive in.

Chapter 2

Duncan with the red hair started larking about one night as he was always doing in one way or another. He held an imaginary microphone in his hand and imagined that he was some famous singer; then he put on a dress over his jeans and swung around the wallbars. While this was going on, the piano roared out, spitting, emanating forth *Chopsticks* and other simple tunes. After some time, he, not liking, or being a strange sort of extravert, feeling embarrassed or having a persecution complex about his red hair, had it dyed black. I, at that point, also desired to dye my own jet black.

Outside the gym was a black and white abstract mathematical design, which reminded me of piano keys. There were prints of famous paintings all over the Unit. In the corridor, outside the door to my room, were prints of a Picasso and the Modigliani. Farther up the corridor of the Boys' End was a print of the Mona Lisa, or the "Moanin' Liz", as it was known, which annoyed Dave so much that he took it down off its hook off the wall and hid it on top of one of the lockers in the Boys' Locker Room. Dr. Martin and the top brasses didn't notice for about a month, nor did they pay any attention. Dr. Martin, incidentally, had hanging from his wall a surrealistic painting entitled *Henry VIII I Am I Am*, which he chose himself.

Other paintings included two scribbled paint-splashers, one a nude and the other a still life, both done at art college by the daughter of an ex-nurse of the Children's Unit. There were also prints of a Paul Klee, a fertility goddess, which people thought was supposed to be the Virgin Mary, an African statue of another fertility goddess ("The Titty Woman"), plus many original paintings by local artists including, eventually, myself, and, of course, our head teacher.

Dave and I took an interest in art and music. We, or I by myself, often sat in the Visitors' Room listening to the radio or playing chess, and I often sat there by myself reading books, including a lot of poetry. One time, much later, he and I went to see an art exhibition in the village nearby (which was very good) and he and I, on the way back, walked together talking about astronomy and other things very loudly when two girls, walking in the opposite direction, repeated what I was saying and laughed at it.

The paintings we did were good, though. They were a complete expression of, and also made me forget about, other things in my life. Our head teacher, who was himself an artist, said to me that some of the paintings were very remarkable and that he might at some time exhibit them somewhere without names to communicate with other teenagers who had felt similar to what we had felt. I wonder if he has done so yet. I sincerely hope he has.

Often I had mental excursions with girls and other kids, when taking walks. Laughing or shouting out strange things. I wondered, "Do they like me, or do they think, 'Maybe he's from the loony bin?'". These were the sort of times when I wasn't sure what people were thinking about me and thought that they were all looking at me. Once, on a week's holiday home, I passed the local Junior Secondary School. On the village green, outside the school, the boys were having a games lesson. The games master blew his whistle to call them back in, and for ages I couldn't get these guilty feelings out of my head. The whole village, or even the whole world, knows about me being in a mental hospital – my parents have written to the newspapers and now everyone knows that Tony Whitfield is the most abnormal inhuman psychopathic lunatic that the world has ever known. Imagine what it is to feel that you are the sickest person in the world and that everyone in the street will look at you and recognise you and stare at you with eyes full of hate, but at the same time being too polite and nice to tell you that they hate you which makes it a hundred times worse. But you are public enemy number one and they will talk about you and your evils and your madness and your stupidity behind your back day and night. Ah well, so it goes, and we don't care about hurting your feelings and will stare and penetrate you with unnatural incestuous black magic evil eyes.

And, at times when these feelings were at their strongest, I would shout out loud and scream.

Deirdre the asthmatic walked into the dining room for breakfast one morning. She poured out her tea which she spilt over her cup as usual, and drank it disgustingly out of her saucer, coughing and spluttering breathing awkwardly and ranting on to people.

This particular morning, later on, I walked into the girls' sitting room and stared out the window at the frost on the ground this wintry morning of nurses eating their breakfasts of toast that we weren't allowed to have, cleaners, food van drivers, electricians, the Principal Nursing Officer arriving and talking to the nurses over breakfast, then the psychiatrists including Dr. Martin arriving for the Assembly, then the teachers and, of course, the patients. "Since you're a patient, you should be patient."

Well, a few days later, and quite a few times after that, I could hear Deirdre going around the place crying her eyes and head out, shouting, "Why has there always got to be worries?" I thought that someone in such a state as that must have found out that they were going to be condemned to Hell.

Around this time, all the patients in the Unit congregated in the boys' sitting room except for one girl, Maria, and myself. The idea was against the discipline of the staff, who they said were running the place like an Army barracks, which was true. It was put to a stop by the charge nurses, who drove us all to our rooms. "Why were two of the patients here left out of your meeting?" asked charge nurse Alan Oldham at the Assembly next morning.

Soon after Johnny Nero had arrived and was settled and had had his beard played with a few times, he started taking us on cycling trips. On about the third or fourth trip, I went with him to his cottage (The School House) to see his wife and six kids, three of whom were adopted and three of whom were their own.

I liked cycling in the winter atmosphere, but felt like Sysyphus going up the hill to the main road. Going downhill was a pleasure, with the view going back including the Adolescent Unit and the rest of the hospital.

I went on two more cycling trips with them after that: one to an auction in the village about five miles away; and the other to the village nearby. I shall always remember the feeling of cycling uphill past cows and trees and sweating till you reach the wonderful Downtown country town high street full of lighted shop windows, Woolworth's, bus station, cinema, stationers, The Temperance Hotel, the post office and then hurrying round the corner past the big mansion past the farm and the railway line to the river, where in the summer we went for a swim and rowed in our homemade boat, down to the other village full of nice girls and the railway station where Andy laid his head on the line to hear a train coming and I shouted, "You'd better watch out, Andy!", while girls stood by and laughed, and that was the deserted village where I bought a carton of raspberries and walked up the road with Marie where we met Mr. Macpherson the night charge on his motor-bike.

These were the days of love and sunshine, yet a feeling of being in prison, but at least it was better than it is now with all this loneliness and isolation.....

About a year after I left the place, I sat in the bus station cafe before taking a bus down to visit the place again, which I'm thinking of doing now, because I can't take my mind off it. I'll wander around the place like a naked ghost plinking the piano, shouting out, singing out hymns for ambulance drivers and teenagers.

Also the time when I was put to bed for a few weeks by the staff because they thought I needed the rest, and they brought me cups of tea which I threw out the window because I couldn't be bothered drinking them, and a jug of orange juice which I drank and took into bed with me to make love to (that was a joke which I started around the Unit and got a good response from Shirley, the night nurse) and the student nurses came in and joked with me: after I came out of bed and started leading my usual Unit life, I wrote a story about a dream I had about being on the back of a motor-scooter which came to a crossroads where all the roads led back to the same town near the hospital, and which was published in the school magazine.

These were the times when I kept eating apples and not finishing them because I couldn't be bothered, and so did Marie, she said, and she had a craze for eating tomatoes and so did her mother. And I would walk out a little outside the front door and try to communicate with the natural atmosphere and Marie would sit on the front step and so the same. I would sit in the Visitors' Room around eight o'clock at night and look out at the sky and at the really bad REAL mental patients up the road, whom we would meet on the pathways when we were out: I would walk through the gardens looking back with nostalgia and looking forward with anticipation and hope.

I would look out my window and consider putting on a jacket, going down to the railway line and throwing myself in front of a train. Once, when I was about to do it, I had put on my jacket, when Daisy the cleaner came in and said, "What are you doing?" and, after she went out, I took it off and didn't bother. I tried drinking turpentine, but I think it was white spirit – anyhow, it didn't do me any harm.

The van trundled through the grounds and brought the disgusting food we ate, or didn't eat if we got away with it, and I did mange to later on.

My appointments with Dr. Martin then were full of depressing thoughts yet, by his way of it, I was "getting better, but not well enough to go home for good".

Anyhow, let's get back to the point where I left off.

The Madhouse of Love

At school, we played many classical records such as Prokofiev's *Lieutenant Kije* and I sat in my room in the evenings drawing abstract line drawings. One of these, which looked like a large letter 'E', I sellotaped to my wardrobe door.

Chapter 3

During that summer, I asked Dr. Martin for a loan of the book which belonged to him by C.G. Jung, entitled *Man and His Symbols*, which he had received as a present from one of his patients in another hospital, who was a doctor. I was very attracted by many aspects of this book. One of the aspects which attracted me most was the illustrations, which included paintings by patients of Jung and the other authors of the book, and by such artists as Chagall, Klee and Paul Nash whose *Landscape from a Dream* made a vivid impression on me. Other aspects included the many references to dreams and mythology throughout the book. These, along with my own dreams, paintings, music and poetry at that time, occupied my spirit.

One of these paintings of mine was of a subject suggested by Johnny Nero, which he said was an idea of Salvador Dali's. This subject was of two gigantic figures, which I meant not to be of particular sexes, wading at sea near the horizon, while between them rose another figure. I later turned this picture into what was considered a mess by covering it entirely with horizontal dashes around the central figure; thus, giving it the appearance of an angel with a halo.

During one of my appointments with Dr. Martin, or "sessions" as we called them, which, at that point, were three times per week (on Mondays, Wednesdays and Fridays at 3.30 p.m.), we discussed the symbolism of this painting. On protesting that the painting was not my creation in essence, he replied that there is an area of the mind where my thoughts are Johnny Nero's thoughts are Salvador Dali's thoughts. In the same afternoon, we also discussed some other symbolism regarding water, including a dream I had had about crossing a river, the legend of the Styx and a photograph in the National Geographic magazine of a scientist's arm covered with a protective glove, which appeared to me to look like a monster's neck and head. The old analyst let his thoughts tick over: "A monster with a head.... a monster with a head.... Well, I think that what this means, Tony, is that this picture gave you the impression of a huge, monstrous genital, which would be enough to frighten anyone."

While I was reading *Man and His Symbols* and *The Power of Positive Thinking* by Norman Vincent Peale, I wrote an essay called *My Beliefs About the Mind*. One of the highlights of this essay was a belief that the feelings of sheaves of wheat about to be harvested are transmitted by mental telepathy between sheaves throughout several nearby fields within a certain radius. A year later, on re-reading this essay, I found it so disturbing that I tore it up, out of fear that it would horrify anyone else who read it.

I had shown it to Dr. Martin and to some of my friends, such as Dave and Vincent, most of whom appreciated it, and I now regret very much that I took such action upon it in a moment of terror.

At another session with Dr. Martin, he showed me a leaflet about a special boarding school called Harris School, advising me to take it to my room to read. On doing so, my thoughts became so preoccupied with it that I forgot to come to the dining room for the tea break at three. At a quarter to four, I went round after everyone else had finished and, having been refused a cup of coffee, became so mad that I involuntarily smashed everything on the trolley in front of me: fifteen cups, a bowl of sugar and a milk jug: after which I was given a cup of coffee and a biscuit and sent to my room.

*   *   *

For two weeks that summer, I went on holiday with my parents to Scarborough. I said that I enjoyed it. It went like a "normal" holiday apart from one incident, and I only once needed to take an extra tranquiliser.

One night, at our hotel, they were holding the weekly dance. I was unsure whether my parents expected me to come to it or not. As they were getting ready for it, I felt more uneasy. I ended up in my room writing a letter to Dr. Martin. I think that he still has it. As I cannot quote directly from this letter, I can only quote from memory. I wrote something like: "Everyone was downstairs having a good time, but I was not.... and I wandered around stark naked and did all sorts of nutty little things like that."

Chapter 4

After I came back from holiday, my personality was changing somewhat. I showed Liz Hart, the night nurse, a new poem and she said that she didn't like this change in me. On the cover of the school magazine, which I designed, I wrote: IF WE GO ON AND ON, ON THE SAME RAILS FOR TOO LONG, WE BECOME SOMEWHAT STALE. I also wrote the following article for the magazine:

THE HAPPENINGS AT THE ADOLESCENT UNIT AT THE FIRST WEEK OF SCHOOL

This is a time for realising old fantasies, if we can. During the last month, before the school holidays, they lay quiescent. Now, when we are preparing to get us back into the routine of school life, it is time to get these fantasies going again.

So, let's get to work! Since we can get lazy and do no work, thus becoming restless. The first thing which we must do is to set a routine. If we do this, we will not be able to find excuses for such idleness. This being done, we can find our way to climb back up the rest of the slope and on to the rails to remain stable with both rationality and emotions.

So we shall have to get working at both the normal schoolwork and the section of school and routine life, which we can use to realise our fantasies: and, presently, after the comparative struggle is over, in our spare time, we can do what we really want to do and what truly fills our minds with flowing tranquillity; thus, along with the rest of the rota, helping to put us into a good mood for as much of the time as is possible – and is necessary.

One of the new admissions was a girl called Vivian Smith. She was put on the dishes with me the day after she was admitted. We talked about why we were there. I talked to her a lot after this.

To begin with, she seemed to be interested in Dave but, one night, I said to her, "You're obsessed with Dave," to which she replied, "I'm no more obsessed with Dave than I'm obsessed with my Dad and that's saying something."

One late afternoon, I asked her if she would like to go for a walk with me. I held her hand.

After this, she came round to my room at nights to talk to me. She told me about the home she had been in, and how cruel it had been to her.

One of these nights, she said that she had something very important to tell me. But she couldn't tell me. Of course, straight away, I knew what it was. The evening dragged on and she talked for ages. She started talking about a boy she used to go with called Ronnie Parks. Eventually, she came out with, "One night, I was drunk and I went home with him... I had intercourse with him." After that, silence for five minutes.

It was nearly ten o'clock, the time when all the lights were put out, and she walked out and went round to her room without saying a word.

The next morning, at breakfast, I spoke to her as usual. She didn't think that I would speak to her after she had told me that.

On Wednesday afternoons, volunteer students from the University came to talk to us. We young people had much more understanding with them than with the staff and needed them to cling on to for inspiration. I could talk to them about poetry.

One of the girl students, Lorna, lent me some poetry books. From then on, she and her boy-friend Dave took a great interest in my poetry and music. In fact, several months later when I was readmitted after having been discharged, they journeyed all the way to the hospital just to see me!

One particular Wednesday night, when Vivian and I were on the dishes, she talked about a woman "up the road" (in the main block of the hospital) who "had been in Melancholy for ten years". I somehow associated this with the Epitaph of Gray's *Elegy*, which we had gone through in school recently, along with Rupert Brooke's *Fishes' Heaven*. While I was explaining to her: "You know how you talk about Melancholy with a capital M......", Bill Mahon, the head teacher, who was on his late evening, walked in to fill his teapot. Bill and Dr. Martin had formed a conspiracy with the rest of the staff to keep us apart because "our relationship was bad for us". This really made me despair. In fact, combined with being kept indefinitely imprisoned, it made me want to kill myself.

It was growing dark. When the train passed, I shuddered, trembling at its penetration into my brain. I knew that there was only one woman on the train who was the same kind of person as I was.

Vivian said that she thought that I was the reincarnation of a boy who was killed by a train at 16. As I have said, I would often sit in my room at night in hospital and contemplate committing suicide by running in front of one of the trains which rolled by every ten minutes.
It was one of these nights that remind you of witches and warlocks, and around Halloween. I wandered down the road by the hospital. The trees and cars reflected on my coat. I took my trousers down, and then took my shoes and socks off. Having crossed the road, I passed the farm, climbed over the stile and quietly wandered down to the river to drown. But, just before making the final decision to do so, I changed my mind.

The Madhouse of Love

I saw a pair of car headlamps coming down the road, standing out like the Aurora against the black sky. It stopped. I recognised the car as belonging to Alan Oldham, the charge nurse. He took me back to the Unit since I had gone for a walk without permission.

I also ate gluttonously. At the coffee break, I would eat half a dozen slices of bread ladelled with butter and syrup, and would keep coming back for another like an alcoholic for his next drink.

I took a shower four times a day. I didn't feel mentally or physically fresh unless I had just had a shower. Basically, I felt guilty, as if I was doing something terribly sick and weird. People didn't seem to notice that I was doing this. Only one boy, a day patient, ever mentioned it to me.

Vivian had a dream that George Rothchild, the head charge nurse, was dressed up in armour leading the staff in a battle against us. I wanted to appear to her as a hero who was making her life better. In my room one night, I wrote a song about it.

In my room, on other nights, I wrote other poems which were different, less organised.

Once, I took a very bad framed picture by an ex-patient, a girl, Janus Spring, and smashed the frame, although I did no damage to the painting itself. I felt very guilty about destroying anything which was meant to be creative. In the same afternoon, I went round to Dr. Martin's office and threw all the files all over the place. He asked me later, "Who flung all my files about this afternoon?"

The electricians went on strike and the darkness seemed to have something to do with the darkness in my life. A joke started that Vivian and I had bribed the electricians to put the lights out. One night, the lights came on, being powered by the hospital generator. We were told to use as little lighting as possible. So, being rebellious to the authorities, I went into the gym, switched on all the lights and banged on the piano.

I started skipping school for the first time. The teacher was very angry, although I was never actually forced to go.

As the staff tended to pick on me, I tended to shout back at them, at which I would be dragged along to bed. Having them physically set upon me, of course, made me much more mad and I would shout and scream ridiculous things and get the intromuscular needle. The effect of this forced me to lie down in order to feel slightly comfortable. I felt all over physically awkward and was advised by the staff, when in such pain, to take a shower. I would usually be up in the evening.

This would happen about once a month, and always on a Friday before my parents came to take me home for the weekend. It was labelled my "manic flight".

On one of these occasions, I took a tumbler from the kitchen to the toilet and threw it on the floor. When George Rothchild heard about it, he told me to sweep it up. I called him a bastard and said that I wouldn't.

Vivian and I would still see each other and speak to each other, but were advised to split apart at times, such as the night when we were found talking in the Boys' Locker Room. I was given lectures to which I would have paid no attention had I had the experience of what people's bad advice can do to one. But I did pay some attention. I decided that I wouldn't see her after I was discharged and dreamed that I would meet another girl who would be better looking; something like a girl I had seen when on holiday with my parents on the Isle of Skye the year before.

In Bill Mahon's art class at school one afternoon, we had a lesson in lino cuts. My hand seemed to go where it would and drew a design which impressed me greatly, but which I thought would be more suitable for an oil painting. I was changing. It impressed Vivian as much as it did me.

On my next weekend home, I became very depressed and longed for Vivian. I wrote a letter to her which ended, "I dedicate my life to people like you". I believed that I would commit suicide soon, so I decided to sell the picture to Alan Oldham before I died. However, by the end of the next week, I decided that he wouldn't appreciate it and took it home at the weekend in the boot of my father's car. During my week at home, I saw a programme on television about Modigliani. It said that he "died at the age of 35 of drink, drugs, malnutrition and tuberculosis". I told Vivian about this when I got back, and said that I was in the same state of mind as he had been in. I brought back my brother's tape recorder and, dropping it, put it temporarily out of order. I got mad about this: screamed and shouted and waved my hands in front of a girl's parents and older sister. I was really worried about what my brother would think of me. Dr. Martin came round, dressed in a sports jacket instead of a suit since it was the weekend, and talked to me, reassuring me by saying that, at the most, all that was broken was a tape recorder and that at least it was not someone's nerves. When I told the others about it and how I was worried about it, they advised me to show it to Dave since he was good with electrical things. This I did, and was glad to find that he was able to fix it.

At this time, I was having a conflict with Dave about art and such things. He drew a pen and ink drawing in Johnny's class of a lock and key, which was supposed to be a sex symbol. This had been mentioned in *Man and His Symbols*, where there was a picture showing a nun turning a key in a lock. At first, I was annoyed at Dave's drawing and said that I didn't like it. However, I later decided that I liked it and asked him if I could have it to hang on my wall. He gave it to me. I then started to accept Dave again. I again started to accept the "scientific" as opposed to the "artistic" side of myself. In the late afternoon and at nights, I worked out mathematical problems in my room. One of these evenings, I was annoyed with myself that I couldn't solve the problem on which I was working. I told Vivian about "my little mathematical thing" and she laughed although she was also perturbed about it. She became excited with me at times when I was really excited about writing poems.

However, my conflicts with Dave still continued. One afternoon, I showed him some of my poems, which he didn't understand. Another afternoon, on showing him a book of poems by e.e. cummings, he replied that he "preferred something nice and down to Earth like science fiction"!

I also read science fiction, however, and took some S.F. books out of the library, and I always remember walking up to the library with him and his girl-friend Mary whom I mentioned earlier in this book. From the top of the hill, on which the main block of the hospital stood, where the library was, one could hear the piano playing in the gym.

By this time, it was October and would soon be Halloween. Vivian was certain that she was a witch, and was going to buy a long black dress which she would wear at the Halloween party, along with a witches' hat and a broomstick. The staff said that she shouldn't do this, but her doctor, Dr. McAllister, a new face in the place, gave her permission. There was a lot of excitement about this spreading around the Unit. She typed me a letter about it saying that we would know each other after we were dead but that we would not know each other as Vivian Smith and Tony Whitfield. I still believe this. I imagined myself committing suicide and coming back as a ghost to make love to her.

One night, we went into the school to paint and listen to records. I drew on the blackboard an image from a recurring dream which I had had as a small child. It was of a white shape, the borders of which were two slanting lines drawing towards the centre, upon a black background. I wrote beside it "BLACK MOONLIGHT" – a phrase with which, in my mind, I associated it. Next morning, when Bill Mahon saw us, he said, "Oh yes, this morning, I had to rub all the black moonlight off the blackboard. People who talk about black moonlight are those who are not content with ordinary white moonlight," and gave us lectures against witchcraft. He told us that he had been to spiritualist meetings and that his mother and his grandmother had been mediums. In the next edition of the school magazine, we changed the first line of Gregg's Halloween poem from "On Halloween night in the pale moonlight" to "On Halloween night in the black moonlight".

We held a séance in the Girls' Locker Room one night with two other girls. Vivian brought in her statue of the Virgin Mary, since she was a Catholic, and a tumbler. The highlight of the evening was when Vivian spelt out

"C...L...A...R...E" and pointed at me. The only thing that this could mean to me was that my grandfather's name was Clarence but was known to most people as Clare. Vivian told me that she saw an old man with a walking stick in the corner, and said to me later that my grandfather must have known a man called Peter Townsend and that he was the old man with the walking stick.

All of a sudden, the door opened and Liz Hart, the night nurse, walked in. She told the other night staff that we were holding a séance in the Girls' Locker Room and split it up.

Liz Hart acted as a postman between Vivian and I at nights. When we were both in bed, I would write a letter and give it to her to take to Vivian. Then Vivian would reply.

One of these times, Vivian said in one of her letters, "There's something I have to tell you, but I feel embarrassed. I love you." I wrote back, "I love you too."

The Halloween party came round. Vivian did dress up in a black dress, a witches' hat and a broomstick. We went out to the bonfire, but she said that she didn't get any pleasure from watching a lot of fire and flying flames.

Strangely enough, I later wrote this weird poem:

```
     FI                              RE
     RE                              FI
     FI                                RE
   RE                                    FI
     FI                                RE
    RE                               FI
     FI                              RE
```

```
   FFFFFF    I     RRR      EEEEEE
   FFFFF     I     R   R    EEEEEE
   F         I     R RRR    E
   FFFFFF    I     RRR      EEEEEE
   F         I     R   R    E
   F         I     R   R    EEEEEE
   F         I     R   R    EEEEEE
```

```
    RE                              FI
   FI                               RE
  RE                                FI
 FI                                   RE
  RE                                FI
   FI                               RE
```

ANYTHING ELSE IS DEAD

I was very perturbed about this after I had written it and
told Dr. Martin about it. I said that I associated it with
something which was very obnoxious and of which I had
a terrible fear – namely, castration. The "black
moonlight" dream I also associated with a flame in
darkness and had worked out a theory about Hell, but
decided, in the end, that the theory about castration was
much more likely. I showed the poem to Vivian, but said

that what I thought it meant was so disturbing that I couldn't tell her, and tore it up.

At this point, some of my other creations also worried me.

I became addicted to the piano. Frequently, in the afternoons after school, I would go over to the piano and literally be unable to come away from it. One time, I played on and on, partly out of tune, and I overheard Dr. Martin saying, "I'd better go and see how Tony is. He's really going at the piano." I told Nurse Andrews that I had been playing a lot of rubbish on the piano, but she said that she didn't think that it was a lot of rubbish, but that it was very good. She was an appreciator of music and could often be seen on a Sunday night, when I arrived back, with her head in her hands listening to a concert on the radio, after she had given the party which she gave every second Sunday night, when she was on duty, with Bircher Müsli and other stranger foods.

Once a day, either in the afternoon or evening, I played *Für Elise*, which was very sad and reflected the sadness in my life.

I remember, on the way home with my mother and father one Friday night, we looked in at "Aunt" Geraldine's. Aunt Geraldine was really my mother's friend. Her husband was unemployed and her daughter, her only child, Norma, was a spastic. Sitting there, I compared her with Vivian. She was still a child, whereas Vivian was an attractive girl, with whom I could have sexual and spiritual communication. I imagined myself living with Vivian in Lossiemouth, a beautiful place where I had been on holiday. While I was thinking this, Aunt Geraldine was talking to my parents about a Marxist woman she had seen on television who said that the Revolution was going to come soon.

The Madhouse of Love

Earlier, in the summer, a new girl called Tina had been admitted. She had liked a poster which I had on my wall and asked me if she could have it; so I gave it to her, since I was tired of it in any case. Paul, one of the boys, standing outside the door, said, "You'll get off with her!"

It was about this time, in November, that we heard that she had been caught behind the mortuary having it off with a boy from Admission (the Admission Ward being the equivalent of the Adolescent Unit for over-18s). Vivian told me that she was bisexual, and, at one time, I heard her say to her, "You're not only a nymphomaniac but you're a lesbian as well!" She was frightened that I was getting the two of them mixed up in my mind about some things they had said or done. She said, "I hope you're not getting me mixed up with Tina!"

Vivian had been talking to boys from Admission and going around with student nurses, all of which I didn't mind.

During my period of "mind-mixing" and so on with Dave, I was determined that I was to have group therapy with him and persuaded Dr. Martin to let us have a session together. This he did, but nothing seemed to come out of it and we said very little, except that I told Dave about how I felt more awake in the morning but felt everything on top of me by the afternoon, to which Dave replied, "That's funny. I've never felt any different from one part of the day to another."

After this, I felt that I would have to have a group session with Vivian, but was told that this would not be possible "because of the staff relations between Dr. Martin and Dr. McAllister".

We both walked along the road to the bus shelter one afternoon, sat down and talked sadly about it. Somehow, it was something that had to be done. I also talked about how I had to get an organ, since I was no longer content with the piano. She asked me, "Do you go to church? You could ask the minister if you could play the organ." I said that I didn't like to answer questions like that. That also seemed like no solution to the problem.

I, by this time, had followed Dave's habit of walking down the corridor naked to the toilet at nights (we were both very tall for our age and fully sexually developed) and Duncan had been put to bed for a few days for jumping naked into the swimming pool, where a van took some of us every Thursday.

Duncan was always playing pranks. One night, I was in the gym thumping out Viking Blues on the piano rendering it to the black night and tape-recording it to the dark outside the huge windows. Duncan and some other boys came in through the woodwork store and stood at the door laughing. I was furious. I jumped, dropping the tape recorder on to the floor. Not knowing what was happening nor what to say at first, I shouted, "Hello, Cheerio," then stormed across the floor, thumping and echoing across the high ceiling, to chase them away. The tape recorder was undamaged, but the whole affair was recorded on the tape. I had a good laugh about it afterwards with Andy and John Pritchard, a boy who was later to be admitted. And Gregg blurted out, "What's THAT?" when he heard all the bangs.

I had heard that I might be released shortly after Christmas. When I went out with Vivian when she had her smoke, I told her about this. (Although there was a rule against smoking, patients smoked outside and the staff turned a blind eye. In fact, the night staff went out for a smoke with the smokers. When George Rothchild was on duty late one night, he saw them with a nurse and shouted to her, "Get round the corner there, where I can't see you!") She said, "Don't go on about it. It might never happen. And if you come back, you'll probably stick a knife in me, or something. Oh, I don't mean that!" Around the Unit, the idea of sticking a knife in someone was supposed to be a sexual symbol.

The students were still taking an interest in my poetry. By this time, I had filled a whole notebook of poems and lent it to Lorna. I was very glad to let anyone read my poems who wanted, and not nearly as shy as some of showing my personal feelings on paper. When Lorna returned them, she gave them to Vivian, who put them on Bill Mahon's chair. Since I was in conflict with Bill, I didn't want him to read them. I almost grabbed the book from him, although I wouldn't have dared to, but excitedly persuaded him to let me have it back, saying that it wasn't I who had put the book of poems on his chair. I laid them down somewhere, and, between that time and half-past three when the school closed, I was terrified, listening from the other room working on the magazine thinking, whenever I heard his voice, that he was reading the poems out loud to the whole class.

Bill Mahon presently took the class to the cattle market. Viv asked me, "This isn't the agricultural show you went to, is it?" This was a joke that had been going around the place. Earlier in the year, we had gone to see the Agricultural Fair which had been held only a few hundred yards up the road. It so happened that it was raining very badly this day, and I had only a shirt on. We went into a tent which was selling food and refreshments. I let John Mackay and Willie Pope slip in front of me, since I was frightened that I would buy something different from them and be embarrassed. Both of them bought a packet of crisps and a shandy. So I bought a packet of crisps and a shandy. They laughed. Steve said, "D'you know what that stuff is?" Being sensitive, I became very annoyed when anyone mentioned this.

Viv and I walked a few yards behind Bill, who wore his hair long behind his bald head, and criticised him, saying exactly what we thought of him, his egotism, his tendency to interfere and be destructive.

Viv told me about Joan, the girl she had shared a flat with. She was an artist and so was her father, and she helped run a crafts shop. Viv wore a bracelet from the shop. Later, she gave me a medallion on a chain which had engraved on it the face of King Edward VII and his wife, and, which, along with her letter and articles for the magazine, is all that I have to remind me of her.

Joan's father was looking for a nude model but couldn't find one, so Joan would have to pose for him. She said, "Well, I wouldn't like to pose for my Dad!"

She described Joan's father's house. He had nude paintings of his wife in the living room and on the side of the stairs.

She also told me about a programme she had seen on TV about an artist who reminded her of me. I wasn't sure what sort of job I would do. I imagined myself painting and I imagined myself doing nothing. I talked to Viv about this. I was anti-education by this time, but I was also averse to, or couldn't imagine myself doing practical or manual work. Bill Mahon and Dr. Martin were confusing me even more about this, as about everything. I was certain that I would somehow leave home and be free.

*   *   *

That night, Helen and Viv were in Dave's room till half past ten. Dave was in his underpants, and I could hear a lot of shouting coming from his room, which was next to mine. I came down the corridor naked, having just had a shower. Helen came out of Dave's room and shouted, "Ah! Tony Whitfield just walked down the corridor naked!"

I stood by the open door so that she could see me as she walked up the corridor.

Viv had talked to me about how attractive and sexual pipes were to her. On the van on the way to the swimming baths, Pete Richards, one of the charge nurses, smoked a pipe "and that was braw" – in other words, it was brilliantly sexual and phallic. She was both frightened and attracted by it. After she had told me about this, when I got the chance, in the staff office at the girls' side, I put Pete's pipe in my mouth.

At this time, my brother Hamish was being persuaded by his girl-friend Shona to start smoking a pipe, to which he succumbed.

While I was in the office with Pete's pipe in my mouth, I went through various daydreams in my mind and carried on to my room to continue these daydreams. They went from one thing to another and then from another to another, then another to another. It is amazing how the mind boggles and flits when allowed to fly free. Dave, who had never been conscious of dreaming, had told me a year before of a "half-dream", of which he had

65

become conscious during the day, where Alexander the Great and some other men had been knocked down into some sort of pit. Dave had been one for such stories. He had taken a book out of the library called *Four Ages of Man* which had been to do with Greek mythology etc. Well, anyhow, when I was having this daydream, I went through many thoughts, and, at one point, someone, who seemed like Gregg, and who, somehow, was a direct descendant of Macbeth, had got sex mixed up with his religion and was locked up and chained with horrible black fences. (We had been doing *Macbeth* at school at that time which had some inspiration or connection with this.) However, a few miles down the shore and beyond, in the dream, was a part where I could swim naked and be seen by everyone in the sea without shame.

This business I, of course, told to Dr. Martin later, along with the business of having had Pete's pipe in my mouth.

That week, I decided to go to the swimming baths, to which I had not been going regularly, since I couldn't be bothered. We went by the usual route – the route during which, on the first time I had gone there shortly after having been admitted for the first time, I had fantasised that I would somehow be set free and discharged. The castle which we passed by had been the object of conversation of Jimmy Todd as we passed. All I remember now was a conflict between Celtic and Rangers supporters. Jimmy Todd's friend was Duncan with the red hair. Duncan, who was a staunch Catholic and strong Celtic supporter had been, at this point, wearing a blue shirt. For any ignorant readers, green is the Celtic colour and blue is the Rangers colour. Alan Oldham had said, "Duncan is wearing blue because he has nothing else to wear." I had thought to myself, "If he has nothing else to wear, why doesn't he wear nothing?" Duncan was, of course, very poor. Both Duncan and Jimmy Todd (whose nickname was Barry Wagstaff) were orphans. Duncan had been brought up as a Catholic, whereas Jimmy Todd wasn't anything as far as I know. Duncan and his brother wore green Irish jackets and Duncan brought in records of patriotic Irish folk songs.

Regarding sex I (?!) first learned the facts of life (flappy drawers) from Dave and Jimmy Todd. I had, in fact, heard the facts of life before from boys and girls at primary school but I wasn't sure whether to believe it.

However, Jimmy Todd, with Dave's employed assistance, to use a sarcastic expression, asked me one afternoon (readers please remember that this was more than a year before I met Viv) if I knew the facts of life. Well, I knew what they were talking about but was not absolutely certain. Jimmy Todd asked, "Do you know what sexual intercourse is?" I had not heard this term before. I said, "No". Jimmy replied, "Have you ever seen a girl stark naked?" I replied, truthfully, "No". He amazed, or, at least, amused by my naivety, attacked, "Have you never seen your sister stark naked?" I had to explain that I had no sisters. "Well, have you ever seen your Mum completely naked?" "No," was the answer. My mother had always been very prudish and puritanical, anyhow. This had a great reflection on when we walked with girl students through local fields that winter, how I became obsessed with beards and how Dave always wanted to grow a beard. He was very physically and sexually mature. The next question from Jimmy was, "Have you ever seen a picture of a girl in a magazine stark naked?" "No." Well, I had seen pictures of girls' breasts naked and had beautifully loved to look at them, but, to answer truthfully had I seen a picture of a girl completely naked, the answer was "No". I had actually looked at girls' tits at primary school, but they weren't very developed.

So they told me about sexual intercourse. They told me about how a girl has a hole and a man puts his cock into her hole and from that comes a baby. I had great pleasure in listening to this. Jimmy said to Mary Langford, one of the nurses listening, whose standard phrase was "I am not amused!", "Well, we've told him about when a man takes a woman for sexual intercourse, but we haven't told him about prostitution or contraception." Mary said, "Well, that's all he needs to know!"

I had heard all this business, which they had described as sexual intercourse, already, except that I was not sure whether to believe it or not. Hamish McBride, a boy I knew at
primary school who stayed across the road from me, had said, "You know, you piss into her arse and that gives her a baby. Don't believe the lies they tell you about putting your cock into her hole."

But the rumour which I had heard before, I knew now to be true. When my mother and father came to take me home that weekend, I felt superior to them since I was now an adult and they hadn't a clue that I knew. From then on, I had brilliant talks and everything with people, except that the psychiatrists and people somehow tried to make things different. If only I had been left alone.....

From then, although I had already founded it anyhow, I founded a deep relationship with Dave. As I have said already, he went on about space travel and about Einstein's Theory of Relativity and how, if you have a powerful enough telescope, you can see the back of your head. And about how there is no such thing as a completely straight line and how things always make a circle eventually. Well I've told you most of the story of that already, and how I first talked to Dr. Martin at the age of twelve, and how beautifully sexually you know what I mean.

At about this time, the first time I ever remember taking a shower, I felt beautifully cold and naked and wet and perhaps almost sexual, an ecstasy. Well, anyhow, I had associated this with Daphne Hoeniker's bare arms on the phone. Daphne was the girl whose wet hair had been pulled over her eyes on the way back from the swimming baths to make her look as if she had hair all around her head, which made an impression on me. Well, anyhow, back to the point where I left off.....

But just one more thing before I go. Rhona, a nurse who knew Ann, but whom I did not like and thought was mindless, every Sunday night, when I came back from my weekend at home, asked me, "Have you had a nice weekend?" At these times, I felt awkward. By my religion, I could not tell a lie and I also wondered whether she was merely making conversation. Ann and I saw her brother in the village, when out for a walk, looking into a bookshop window. One of the book covers showed a naked boy and girl together holding each other. I felt in such ecstasy at seeing this, that people could actually show such beautiful things.

Well, anyhow, back to the point where I left off.....

The point being that, at that time, I masturbated dreams of running along beaches nude with nude girls. Trickcyclist Dr. Martin tried to levitate people in the boys' sitting room in the dark. We talked about life after death and about Freudians, Jungians and Existentialists.

I liked going into the village to buy something with my 10/- birthday present with Mary Thomson, the girl who was in the dream of the black Rolls Royce with the rainbow painted across it, and Ann, and seeing the lights of the town or the city against the hazy sky of winter.

I liked making a snowman out of the snow that year.

Well, anyhow, back to the point where I left off.....

I had decided to go to the swimming baths that week. We drove in the van past various places where I had vainly hoped that I would be discharged and allowed to go home, the castle, ("That's my castle," someone said), the loch and the sweet shop where we bought ice lollies and ate yoghurts from the grocer next door to the dairy across the road.

Viv and I were the first to change. I enjoyed letting her see my powerful semi-nudity as I jumped in the water, when her bikini-top fell off.

When we were back in the Unit that evening, I let her hear me singing. I got her in my room and blurted out, "Blya blya blya blya blya." I talked to myself and sang to myself. Dave next door had once heard me talking for ages in a man's voice and a woman's voice. I had taken piano lessons, but had only sat one exam in music theory as a kid at primary school. I remember walking through the night of St. George's Hotel and seeing all the shops light up.

We walked along the corridor and saw Gregg jumping up and down on his bed like mad and shouting at the pitch of a squeaky high voice, "Knickers! Knickers!

Knickers! Knickers! Knickers!" and Pete Richards walked into the passage and asked, "Who's doing the shouting?"

Gregg was a lad. Every night, the charge nurse from the Children's Unit walked into the dining room and introduced himself by saying, "Evening, peasants!" to which Gregg replied, "The peasants are revolting and there's one revolting peasant!"

Dave and I began to hit it off a bit better. At this time, we both had the habit of sitting in our rooms with the windows wide open. Remember that this was mid-winter. The electricians' strike was still on, and we never felt cold despite the fact that the place was normally centrally heated.

We both grew plants. I only had two, both cacti. One of them wasn't planted properly in the pot and, every time the open window closed with a bang in the wind, it knocked it out of its pot out of the window. Worriedly, I pleaded with Dave to fix it several times.

His room was full of plants of all descriptions including "Grandad's Beard" and "Wandering Sailor".

Dave's girl-friend from a year before had been Daphne Hoeniker. She came back one afternoon to visit, as do all the ghosts from this particular monastery I am writing about, haunting the castle like lost kings and queens. Her eyes showed some real feeling of sexuality as they stared beyond within her and she sat cross-legged on top of the cupboard. Behind her hung our paintings of black bats flying in front of the moon and lively horses jumping in front of the sun in an alien brightly coloured landscape. On the other walls were two murals, one of a stark naked native jumping around dusty ground and, opposite that wall, the other mural was of a handsome face like mine rising above a castle above a dark blue sky. Murals were full of beautiful black eyes staring out everywhere. Freuds, faces, lovers, magnificent patients in flying machines..... Phallic symbols of black arrows.

That night, Daphne disappeared, had not been seen by anyone – psychiatrist, parents – and had apparently been sleeping rough.

Dorothy Walls, a new admission, a cousin of Duncan's, had a conversation with me in front of a typewriter with a typing manual by someone named David Draffen. She asked me if I had any idea why people would want to commit suicide. I replied that I had felt like committing suicide but did not feel like that any more and that, as long as you had life and love in you, you wouldn't want to commit suicide. My heart was full of hope of getting out of the place and living normal relationships with girls and with things like that. I looked forward and didn't feel like committing suicide. Picking up the typing manual, I said, "David Daphne... I mean Draffen." "What on earth are you talking about?"

Out of my hopes and my leaving off my obsession with taking showers, I wrote an article for the December magazine.

We would sit out on the steps of the front entrance talking to each other in our secret language of escaping and sleeping in haystacks. We gave each other accounts of our past lives and things we had got up to. We were fairies in the prime of life, screwing in the religion of psychiatrists, sitting in our rooms, planning to run in front of trains which rolled by every ten minutes.

The Madhouse of Love

On Sunday nights, when I came back with my parents, Duncan would be sitting on the front step smoking with two or three others.

One night, Duncan was smoking with others, including Viv, out the back. They were outside the window of the boys' toilet. I was having a shower, but the water was too cold so I would, in the instances of the water being too cold, climb on the pipes and turn a tap by the sinks, above which were the windows. I hoped that some woman would see me naked through the windows and the window of the woodwork room on the other side of the outside passage where they were smoking.

Later, Vivian asked me, "Were you taking a shower or something a minute ago? All we could see was this hand coming out the window. It was really gruesome."

Artlessly, I would take one shower a day and wash my clothes once a week in the laundry room. I felt satisfied in making the effort to do these things regularly. I would think silently in the laundry room, while everyone was shouting outside and Ravel's *Bolero* echoed from the school.

When photographs were taken, they were developed in the same room and the linen cupboard next door was used as a darkroom. These were the times of morose silent thinking, while I imagined the photographs making me famous, such as in a book or poetry or in the papers. I once had my photo pinned on the notice-board, which was fame in a small way.

Dave had always, for some reason, not wanted to go to the swimming baths. His introspection somehow seemed to be nothing much to do with knowing other people. I don't know how or why beings come to know each other. It is just a thing. It is just one of these things. In Hyde Park a few years later, I imagined everyone not wearing clothes and no-one bothering. I walked past streets for Bed and Breakfast to see where I could stay for one night.

During December, one phenomenon preoccupied our minds: the Christmas concert. Everyone was ready to do their own thing and emanating forth, masturbate their drunken, warped personalities upon the audience of one hundred or thereby. I was going to play the piano and sing: *Für Elise* and *Viking Blues*.

These were the days when my mind flipped through Largactil Mogadon the masturbating nite of cows bursting with milk, stars, psychopaths, a bottle of cider on top of a wardrobe, random paper and cardboard on top of the wardrobe, love, talks about suicide, pianos ("Stop making such an obscene noise at this time of the morning!") and making love to the nurses in the childlike shower-taking, seer-sucking, comic-reading, dreaming, night-charge nurses sleeping on the couch night.

Going to the seaside with one's parents with a black jacket on, swimming in the natural phenomenon of a dream masturbating sea, looking at girls' bikini tops falling off, loving and fluffling one's tail on the ground. Oh, what a caffuffle! If only everyone could make love for ever and their minds could be filled with love! Go through the forest with your evil eye.

Speaking of forests, at this point, at nights, I wandered through the dark forest and took my clothes off, then put my coat on top of myself without any shirt or sweater on. I thought that teenagers in the village were looking at me, noticing this. I told Daisy the cleaner that I walked through the woods when I went for walks at night. Oh, I wouldn't go there alone in the dark!

But what a life! Not having stripped to people all that much, I took every opportunity that I could. That was the same forest in which Willie Pope had talked to the cows through the fence and to Johnny Nero about "French letters". Oh, the television is goggling on next door and my mind flits back through the masturbating night to the wood by the monastery like a ghost. Everyone, or, at least, I ate slices of bread and marmalade in the mornings and enjoyed them.

I would wander through the black hospital night for extra medicine when Betty MacGreggor, the night nurse would say, "God bless your little cotton socks!" and "Cigarettes and whisky and wild, wild women – they drive you crazy, they drive you wild!"

Johnny Mathers would run around the Unit in his pyjamas, shouting at the pitch of his voice. He was called "Mental Mathers".

Nostalgia. The hospital at night reminded me of the general hospital I had been in for brain tests. I was probably the only person in Scotland, or, at least, the only person within my circle of friends who knew what my I.Q. was.

I love to screw myself like this.

Dave understood me. Viv understood me. If only I could have stayed with them. I loved them – I truly did. They loved me. Why must people be cruel and shut you out of the sitting room where you masturbate on the couch in front of Martina sitting, saying how "I was great!" What a beautiful thing to say to me!

I would sit in bed, reading the music papers, wondering what would become of me and my love.

Martina was a quiet girl who never ate. I liked this business. What a way to live! Sleepwalking and sleeping, not remembering one's dreams, while Alexander the Great!

I feel now like trying to contact Vivian, taking hold of her and persuading her to leave her husband and come with me.

How I would take walks regularly every afternoon through the hospital grounds, through trees, past fields, past cars and lorry drivers getting out and asking me directions.

I loved sitting in the gym, communicating my piano-playing with teenagers watching astronomy programmes on the television, talking about Freud and suchlike, while Dr. Martin would say, "If Mrs Brown walked in, she would think we were sitting rather close together today, wouldn't she?" Mrs Brown was the typist.

I talked to kids about such sexual permeating loving loony thoughts normal having girl-friends and boy-friends thoughts, séance thoughts, sitting with girls in locker room thoughts, looking at paintings in the staff office and thinking how I should be set free thoughts, nude thoughts, beautiful thoughts, such thoughts as occupied our minds.

I may as well flit on for a moment to the time just before I managed to have myself set free.

Three girls, including one very sexy-looking girl, Doreen, with long, black hair, came round to my room when I was in bed and took all the covers off me where I was sleeping naked.

Then, on the day that I left, they took all the clothes off me and put a dress on me.

Well, back to the point where I left off.....

Viv had written a long poem to me about washing her hair, saying that, now that she had washed her hair, she "couldn't unshampoo her hair". She sent me this letter. Wasn't that quite a business?!

We put on the concert. During it, Johnny Nero wandered in wearing a white coat, absolutely against his unconventional nature.
I played *Für Elise* and *Viking Blues* as planned. Everybody loved it. The students came to talk to me afterwards about how well I had put on my performance. I was the well-loved musician and poet of the place.

Jimmy did his ventriloquist act. Gregg did his "Swami Magammy" magician's act. He said, "Here I hold in my hand a ..... piece ..... of ...... paper." That was part of his "Swami Magammy" magician's act.

Lorna and her boy-friend Mike sat in the audience. Mike was wearing glasses, a jersey and jacket.

When I went home for Christmas, there were rumours that I might not be back, so Viv gave me a copy of the December magazine in case she might not see me again. The night I went, she was discussing forming a suicide pact with Joan and her boy-friend, the charge nurse Bill Whittington. But I remember, at the concert,

Jane looking out the window with Daf the student at the dark black night asking him to have it off with her.

My two weeks at home. This was the period when I thought and thought of breaking free and forming normal relationships with girls at High School.

I wrote a letter to Viv during the holiday, and two to Vincent. On asking my grandmother for stamps, she expostulated, "You can't go writing to all and sundry like that!", but gave me them all the same.

My brother Hamish, who became engaged to his girl-friend Shona during the holiday, was a student and did temporary work for the Post Office, sorting the Christmas mail to get some money so that they could buy a new car. He saw my letter to Viv and, when he came home for dinner, said, "Been writing letters, have ya?" and then remarked, "And there was one to Vincent as well!"

I remember: sitting at the tea table: looking out the window of the upstairs sitting room at the black night, with the cars flashing their headlamps coming down the road towards us; traffic trundling by; thinking about sex and normality and taking baths; everything; going to see people that we knew at New Year and being given drinks from them; Viv saying, "White is pure and virginal," and my replying, "So that's why you wear black!", sitting with my brother Hamish in the sitting room by the white painted table.

My parents' car trundled through the night and I walked up the steps towards the beautiful house, and climbed up the stairs in bare feet looking out at the starry sky and came down to watch television and ate biscuits and cheese and drank coffee self-indulgently till I had had my fill, looked in the mirror, or at my reflection in the ash tray advertising beer, and admired myself. My hair was white and gloved with asylums, science fiction, HP sauce, hospitals, nurses, fairy princes, desserts, desert rats, Antarctica, the moon, love, beauty and *The Planets* Suite. Leaning on the storage heater, I would imagine taking a trip to Mars. I would still love to do so! (While honey-making, bee-keeping, respectable, shaven, mad-sonned parents' friends vanished out the back door), I talked to myself. Oh ..... Oh, God!

This reminds me of the time after I was discharged when I looked out the window and saw a cat's eyes staring at me. I was sure that the cat was an omen meaning that I was about to have a regular girl-friend and I chased the local girls I met when out for a walk, who laughed at me, but didn't know how to act with them.

My brother was looking very sad and sick and later Dr. Martin said to me privately, after my brother and parents had visited me in my room, having been readmitted, "If I had been brought into the room as a complete stranger and asked which of these two boys had had a mental illness, I think I would have said your brother. He goes about in such a dream! What a way to go about life!"

My brother and I were going through strange sort of times with our girl-friends, and I didn't know why, or if it was our parents' fault as such.

I got a birthday present from Hamish and Shona of a nice poloneck jumper which, after that, I wore every time they came to visit. I thought that I looked very sexy in it.

At the above-mentioned time, when Dr. Martin had talked to my parents and my brother in my room, I later went out for a walk with them. Hamish saw a mole coming out of a hole. That was the subject of a lot of the conversation.

We walked past the hospital farm and the sewage works, and I thought of a book of poems by Leonard Cohen which I had been given as a present from Hamish and Shona, which were very sad and reflected the sadness in my life.....

Reading science fiction books alone in my room, dreaming of school, space, Viv, Shona and Hamish, how I looked for friends later on and never found them and tried to manipulate situations.....

Once, during this time, when I was telephoning someone..... I can't remember who...... and had finished trying to frame my latest painting (my third oil painting, the second being the one Viv and I had loved with), I shed tears thinking how sad life can be and that, no matter what the way out was, even if it meant committing suicide, love still reigned and God still loved on us.

I remember the doctor across the road, to whom I was to be transferred. I remember..... my brother, everything and laughing out of love at beautiful nurses and people.

I thought that I should make more normal friends. The first on who I landed was Simon Olding, son of a friend of my father's who used to stay across the road from us and whom I had seen grown-up only once, six months before. I had a hard time persuading myself to tell my parents that I wanted to go to see him the day after New Year's Day.

The Madhouse of Love

My attitude was: "I'll wait until I've sharpened a few more pencils; then I'll ask!" – "I'll wait till this car comes down the road; then I'll ask."

But I did eventually go to see him. He had many friends and was an extravert sociable who worked in his old man's shop on a Saturday morning, and became cheesed off and lay down on his couch unshaven with two jumpers on in the winter. He was the sociable extravert, just as Vivian was.

I never met his girl-friend, but she was a sociable extravert as well.

I would sit with Viv in the sofa of the night and dream of Simon Olding and say that he was the only true person I had met who accepted me for what I was. I also said that he looked like me, which was true. This joke went around, when people saw me, they said, "Simon Olding! Simon Olding!"

That, and the shandy at the agricultural show. And being very close to the doctors before I rebelled and sitting next to Dr. McAllister at the group therapy in the mornings, spouting out "psychiatric jargon". Staring out the window at the moon and my new life of sex. My electrical sexual self coming back from the Christmas holiday. I would look at myself in the mirror for about an hour a year before in my red poloneck jumper. When I took it off, I wondered if it was too cold and wintry to do so, but I was very hot. I drew my self-portrait and other drawings in my room. Dave drew very realistic pictures of nude girls in his notebook, and nude boys as well.

I went along and played Mozart's *Rondo* on the piano to an audience of kids and staff. Then I would play *The Blue Danube* and they would all waltz about.

I walked over to the Children's Unit with Ann and that, somehow, made a deep impression in my mind. The moon rose in the twilit night as we were sitting at the back of the Children's Unit looking at the field, and she would keep saying that she was thinking very much about life. At that time, I spent much of my time wondering how animals felt, so asked her, "So you mean human life?" She talked about all the things she would like to do in her life but didn't have the chance to do. She had been pushed into the course at art college by some teachers at school, and she described how one night she went and sat in a graveyard and wept, as she realised that this was not what she really wanted to do.

I would look out the window at tractor drivers.

Speaking of my electrical sexual self, one night, when we were sitting at the piano, which had been moved into the dining room, Helen Richards asked to everyone, "Don't you think there's something sexual about Tony Whitfiled?", to which I replied, "I've been thinking that for years!" and Vivian exclaimed, "You're about as conceited as that Dave!"

We had to do essays at school. They were of various titles such as "The Tuesday Afternoon Essay" and "The Adolescent Unit", or else "The Greatest Event or Non-Event of the Easter Holidays".

I would paint country cottages in the distance or crofts and farms and ploughed fields. I imagined living in the tribe in Britain who used to wear blue dye and no clothes.

I was released two weeks after coming back from the Christmas holidays. The day of my discharge I was playing the judge in Brecht's *The Caucasian Chalk*

Circle in the woodwork store to the audience of the Children's Unit. I was wearing a tail coat, make-up and a shirt turned back to front with a slip of paper stuck in the collar. There was an encore, but I took my make-up off before the encore so I had to be made up again.

When I tried the tail coat on for the first time, before we drove in the bus to a schools' art exhibition, I tried to put it on on top of my overcoat. On the way to the exhibition, Viv asked me on the bus, "Do you mind if I smoke?" I replied that I didn't mind other people smoking.

I was released. I was free. I was going to run down the school road in the bus with hot piano music licking out the radiator, the *1812 Overture* of sexual delights, love and simplicity.

This reminds me of something I wrote or said to Dr. Martin.

Well, for a few weeks, Dr. Martin and the teachers were deciding whether to put me to Lawrence High School or the local Junior Secondary. I was alone with my hopes and thoughts of flying to Mars and Gustav Holst's *Planets* Suite.

I had a few friends at that point. I had Janet Robertson, whom I went up to see once or twice and played my musical compositions on the piano to her. Also, I lent her a notebook full of poems.

My brother Hamish took me one afternoon to see round the university and students' union. I studied all sorts of faces and glasses. All sorts of people looked at all sorts of notices on notice boards. The bridge stood in the distance over the water near the station where the horns played the *1812 Overture* in Hamish's flatmate's dream. He took me to see his flatmates – typical middle class bourgeois. Hamish and Shona drove me to the Unit in their new Mini car.

The *1812 Overture* flatmate was the only friend of my brother's out of whom I could get any sense. He was also a poet, and was studying psychology and philosophy. Hamish told me later of how one of the philosophy professors used to shout out in the middle of his lectures, "I can't stand it any longer!" and run out, and how a psychology professor was seen sitting in the park talking to the flowers. That was University life. That's where a bloke gets drunk on a Friday night, gets in his car and usually ends up down about Wales or somewhere. That's where a guy gets up in the Halls of Residence in the middle of the night and plays the bagpipes.

At this point, my mind went back to a time when I was sitting on the chest of drawers in the four-bedder staring out the window at the rain, and somehow my mind was changing.

It was decided that I was to go to the local Junior Secondary school until the Easter holidays, which were only in a few weeks' time, to see how I got on, and then I would probably go to Lawrence. By this time, I had sent Mr. Alexander the rector of Lawrence examples of my music, painting and poetry. These were later given to Janet Robertson, who was a pupil there, to bring back to me.

I hoped to mix in with this ordinary school. I hoped, but I, unfortunately, considered myself superior. I am not one for giving advice, but one piece of advice I will give is don't consider yourself superior to anyone and don't let your intelligence if you have any, or stupidity if you have any, be a barrier between you and other people.

I realise this now. Unfortunately, I didn't realise it then. I went for one day and felt out of place with these children who hadn't loved. I know now that I was in love with Vivian but since, at the time, I had never been in love before, I couldn't possibly know. All the time that I was at home, I knew that there was something missing. I remember with my whole heart the village green and the school playground.

Next morning, the alarm bell went. I was going to get out of bed in ten minutes. Within five minutes, my father was at my door shouting, "Tony! It's time to get up!" Because of that, I couldn't. I couldn't get up for my Daddy to go to this rotten school, so that I could take "O" levels and "A" levels so that I could get a degree and be a lawyer or a doctor and own two cars and be worthy of typical middle class life.

If it had happened now, I would realise that rebellion means nothing if you are happy or, at least, have peace of mind in yourself.

However, unfortunately, one doesn't have the experience at the time one needs it – a regrettable fact which almost proved to ruin my life.

That afternoon, I had to telephone Viv to ask her to break into the medicine cupboard and send me enough tablets to kill me. I couldn't do it from my parents' telephone, as my mother would hear. So I walked up to Janet Robertson's house and, explaining the situation, asked politely if I could phone. When Shirley answered, I asked if I could speak to Viv. When she came to the phone, I said, "I want to take an overdose," which she misheard as, "I've taken an overdose." I was cut off. She left the office and went back to washing the dishes. She involuntarily dropped the plates which she had in her hand and burst into tears. George Rothchild came in and assured her, "You don't need to cry just because you've broken the plates!" She explained the situation.

After having been cut off, I telephoned for a second time, again asking to speak to Viv. Janus, who answered, said, "I think you should speak to Dr. Martin." I shouted "No!" and slammed the receiver down.

Desultorily, I walked home.

My father had recently crashed his car and had been given tranquilisers by the family doctor. I knew where they were kept, so, the night before, I had put them in my pocket, gone to the bathroom, locked the door and I had had them all on my tongue, but was overcome by fear that what I was doing was wrong and unnatural. I sat on top of the electric heater, reflected over the past year, and thought that this must be my life's natural end. I spat most of them into the sink, but did swallow some – about fifteen.

My mother gave a sigh of relief that I was alive when I arrived home and Dr. Ramsgate, the family doctor, was there. The escapade had been reported to Dr. Martin, who had telephoned through. I was taken back in an ambulance, my mind reflecting in a daze of wonder, awe, love, hopelessness and transcendence. I tried to hit my head against the ambulance window.

On arrival, I tried to give a short explanation to Dr. Martin in the Visitors' Room. My father went straight back to work, but my mother stayed and I was put to bed.

A new patient, Martin, who had brain damage and whom everyone laughed at, came in that night and played his radio at full volume. I was glad that he came in, that I had someone to talk to. I felt as if I was dead, or being reborn.

Chapter 5

A couple of days later, I got up. A specimen of homo sapiens perambulated in my door, namely Vincent. We had a talk, during which species of time he betokened me with a gilted present, namely *The Moonstone* by Wilkie Collins, of which I read only a few pages. Deeply, I remonstrated the geezer that I must bring my abominable carcass to have an hour's rest in bed, by Harley Street doctor's orders.

My drawing in a black frame, which looked like a comic strip, was on my wall.

There were no curtains, since the hamsters ate them in the instance of having been starved by their owners.

So, at night, I stared out over the beautiful natural landscape. The moon rose and the Hobyas came out. I was in the spare room since I was an emergency case and all the other rooms were full.

Everyone loved me. Viv and Mary came in to see me and said that I was looking much better. I lied to them that I had really taken an overdose, and had been in a coma.

Next day, I went on one of the Unit walks with old geezer Pete Richards. Dr. Martin said that, although I was supposed to be in bed, he was glad that I wanted to mix with them. I sexually intercoursed the piano into people's ears like archetypes flowing up your kilt with a thistle.

The Madhouse of Love

I became lazy to take a bath these nights. It was part of my "up and about" nature to stay up as long as I could these nights, and that was sexual.

I ate marmalade a lot and drank water a lot.

I tapdanced, bumped into people and wiggled my thighs to my own songs of jazz under the floor and swept the floor with wallbars and wrung out the dishcloth on the floor! How interesting!

Viv was sadly to leave. About a couple of months after this, it spread around the supper table, at which sat Mary and Marie, that she was getting married the following Saturday. The day she left, we put on the play *The Hobyas* in the gym. I had to get into bed with Sonia the new girl (who was the old woman). The hobyas had their arms and feet splashed with paint and wore cardboard costumes. I had flour in my hair to make it look white and washed my hair about six times that day to get it out. The departure of Vivian of my life was marked by everyone going out the front door and waving good riddance with green feet.

During Easter, it rained and rained. Life was a depressing rain of Monopoly and card games, and Vincent came to visit in the middle of this. "I'm glad you're feeling better!" he said, the thinking of running in front of a train, still dreaming normal girl-friends, funniness such as a patient not seeing very well kicking his daft glasses on and playing chess with Pete Richards. What a daft old laugh!

I walked down the corridor and threw up my fist in left-wing force to a mixed toilet life. I used the girls' bogs once.

My boots were falling to bits, so my blasphemic parents trundled down one rainy night with my black shoes. I had my others in at the cobblers. I remember trundling in in the depressing rain. Magically, I dreamed of other girls and rapped on the piano to the annoyance and concupiscence of that Dr. Martin son of a bitch. Long were the days, and dark were the colours of my mind in the jungle without no bush telegraph to normal unperverted selves of nonmalfunction or pathological circumstances.

I stood in the wardrobe, with the paper and cardboard store on the top, and thought of death, sex, wet hair.

My black shoes were all right to go up for a walk to the main hospital and watch the bitch feeding its young or bring library books up or stare in the windows of the Admission Ward of the main hospital. I remember looking through the window of the Admission Ward to stare at a dark-haired patient and post a letter to Vincent.

The greatest and least tearful event that happened at this time was, so to speak, well, let's say, the admission of Marie. She trundled through the night without a home and slept under a haystack, alone of otherwise. Ugly but beautiful, I could communicate with her, not fearfully or tearfully her beauty hit my balls with a gust of wind.

Nights were full of dreams of suicide and fame. Days were full of talks and walks with beautiful Mary and Marie. Evenings were full of eating cakes or scones and drinking glasses of milk, and making love to the stars, or a jug of orange juice.

Mightily, I appeared on a movie film taken by Pete Richards, prancing around with Marie.

The Madhouse of Love

I would oft walk out cool nights by myself down to the river or railway or just around. Andy came with me one night and, as I stepped on an empty cigarette packet, I thought of my life and the blue twilit night.

I thought of how a few hundred patients in a mental hospital was a very small number compared to the rest of the world, and how many normal people there are.

We went to the pictures with the students on Friday evenings and swam in the cold sea at night.

We went on walks past the hospital farm and the slaughterhouse, and through fields of bleating sheep feeding the first lambs of spring.

Two new boy admissions were John Mallet and Dave Greenfield. The former thought in turn that he was Jesus Christ and Frankenstein, while the latter weighed 26 stone and had himself put on a liquid diet.

They ran away together and played cards in the woods, and were not seen for several days. I talked to them about it later, over a game of cards.

We talked about euthanasia, food, suicide, poetry, headshrinkers and, of course, sex.

John had an obsession with building his body up and used to buy health foods and feed us all with beautiful apples and pineapples.

We cycled up to the Admission Ward to see Duncan, who had been readmitted there. He, after having taken a shower, had his head spinning round and was a-raring to be discharged. He had just lost his job for about the fiftieth time.

We cycled and perambulated here, there and everywhere to do this, that and the other. We were visited by interesting clowns, social workers, bishops and police. Almost everyone was there. Students of all sorts, eccentric mothers and fathers and, most of all, loving patients.

When my parents visited me every weekend, my heart beat fast with nerves of sexual repression. I went to the village with them to have a meal, or else we would go to the seaside in the summer.

I would again stare up at the main hospital full of loonies. Marie and I once walked up to the main hospital. We met a patient called Jack Parsons up there who made remarks about her low-necked dress and bare legs, and roared madly with laughter falling over himself for ages.

Jack Parsons was well known around the hospital. He went around all day washing cars.

Once, he had run away with a woman patient and slept with her and had sex with her under a haystack.

Another patient was Ian Macpherson. Ian had started working in the hospital as a nurse and ended up as a patient.

Walking up to the public telephone once, I met an old woman who asked me several times, "Is there pictures, or?"

Later on in the year, going up with a girl, I asked an old patient who was staring at us, "What are you nosin' at?", to which he replied, "What the fuckin' hell are you bein' so cheeky for?", which frightened poor Sylvia out of her wits. She clung on to me, and pleaded with me not to speak to them again because she was frightened of these men. These murderers and rapists and psychopaths and religious fanatics who were given jobs washing latrines.

While the "evening peasants" continued, we built a kiln for pottery. I would go out in the morning to help with my jacket on and my hair blown, feeling too cold and worried to protest.

This all happened during the spring and summer. The autumn changed things, making me think more about coping with normal people and jobs and things.

I wrote to Mary when she left. This correspondence was to continue for a year and a half, in a haphazard way. That was Mary who told Marie and I the tale of her aunt's neighbour who frequently took off all her clothes in the middle of the street and conducted the traffic with a Bible. She was always in and out of the lunatic asylum for this reason.

When Andy left, he stole boxes full of things from the school including odd things such as Maths books. I gave him a present of my comic strip drawing. I mentioned something about touching something and he said, "I wouldn't mind touching that if it was real!" about a picture of a girl in a bikini on the front of a magazine on the table in the Visitors' Room where we were at the time.

When Marie left, she stole two recorders.

The new girls sexily loved me. At this time, I ran around the corridors, shouting, "Hello, hello, hello, hello, hello!" I've told you most of the rest of the story about them stripping me naked in bed and putting a dress on me on the day of my final discharge. I wish now that I could have loved one of them at the time.

Every time someone was admitted or discharged, or had their birthday, we had a party or, at least, a tea party with loads of cakes, although sometimes we had dancing.

On my farewell party notice saying, "Goodbye and good luck Tony", one of the girls, Doreen, wrote, after she signed her name, "Your so sexy XXXXX". I really loved that, since I fancied her a lot.

When I came back to visit, I joked with Sheena, one of the other girls who had been there at the time at Vincent's rewelcoming-in party. We forged Dr. Martin's signature and put kisses after it. Dr. Martin wasn't married, and was in his fifties.

Anyhow, back to Mary and Marie. Marie always loved me and ran after me with my poetry, which relieved her depression to a certain extent. While the Nurses' Home looked bleak in the rain like a prison, we journeyed together to the opposition of nurses.

I remember when you played *Chopsticks* on the piano and I swung from the ropes in
 the gymnasium
I remember the time you yattered on about Einstein's Theory of Relativity and I listened
I remember the time when you played Chinese Patience and I stared out the window
I remember the time when you put on your coat and waited for the train.

The Madhouse of Love

I remember the time when your friend put on her duffle
coat to go and see a woman of
   some sort far away
I remember the time when I talked about having mental
telepathy with trains and we ate
   the same cake and praised it!
How fantastic!
I remember the time when you put on your low-necked
dress and we walked up to the
   asylum and the old man shouted "ho ho ho ho ho" and
we looked through the window
   and a man jumped up and laughed and looked at us
I remember the time when we walked past the sewers
I remember the time when we walked in the darkness
together
I remember the time when I was going to put on my coat
at night and hitch-hike along the
   road to the sea and drown myself – I tried to drown
myself once – it was cold and I only
   had a shirt on and I came back something drove me
back I nearly fainted I screamed
I remember having philosophies
I remember shouting out in a classroom "have a
banana"
I remember coming back from a long walk one winter's
evening
I remember showing you poems
I remember taking a shower four times a day
I remember morons interrupting me recording some
music and I shouted and dropped the
   tape recorder off the piano
I remember running outside naked one morning
I remember we had all these pieces of apparatus lined
up for a show of some sort I
   remember having a small summer sports with our
teachers talking and some old friends

coming to visit and having lunch outside and me full of
life and love – oh, these poems –
oh I remember writing poems then oh, these poems .....
I remember very vividly many things – I remember
reading *The Rime of the Ancient Mariner* and writing
Rage
I remember at 2 o'clock in the morning reading two
pages from *The Canterbury Tales*
I remember taking my case from home and emptying all
the books, jerseys, Burns
Treasuries, nightclothes I forgot and never wore
   and I remember sticking paintings on the back of my
door
I remember you smoking outside there and me coming
outside sometimes and saying
   something and joking and being frightened being very
frightened of talking about love -
   everybody was joking and I never came to ..... I never
came to the Christmas school
  party
I remember doing drawings during the night; and all of
these things now are
                                    gone
I remember drawing and my teacher looking at my
drawing
I remember climbing a hill and a friend only wore
slippers
                             eternity awakes
I remember sticking posters on my wall with Plasti-Tak I
had nightmares about it
  afterwards
I remember painting a man with his hands in the air in
the darkness in the classroom at
  night with the hills round about
I remember you sitting talking about
  Rasputin the mad monk
  washing your hair

The Madhouse of Love

Christ, I wish I was back
in these days again!
            for certain reasons
        you feeling nice,
            which was feminine
        and not masculine
        as that pig thought
    me performing my
        songs to people
    someone washing my hair
        him showing a woman round
    saying "it's not exactly the best time
                to be shown
        when you're having your hair washed"
    and her saying "it's not often
        I meet a poet!"
        you saying I was bloody mad,
            that was great!

With white hair, glasses and a pipe, Dr.Martin had sessions with me in a Freudian way. He was also Marie's doctor, and I took another loan of *Man and His Symbols* from him to sub-lend to her, which he didn't like. He took it back.

How I'd hang around behind the barn sipping lemonade, how I'd fly back to the place to see it in sexual frustration, how I'd hang around in cafes reading and thinking.

I knew someone whose sister died of an overdose of Largactil, after going to see her psychiatrist.

I didn't die.

But, after I got out, I didn't find a girl-friend. I had no friends. I was so frightened of people.

I spent a year and a half in suicidal depression.
Then, I left home with 50p in my pocket. Yet, despite my poverty, when the bus stopped on the way down to London, I bought a cup of tea to calm my nerves.

Chapter 6

I went along to the local mental hospital to see if there was an Adolescent Unit, out of nostalgia, and to see if I could relate to the kids and perhaps, if I was lucky, to be able to run away with a girl and hide her in my room.

It was already growing dark.

When I arrived, there was a huge wall in front of the place. I walked all along the wall until I found the main entrance.

Stealthily, I walked in. I came to a signpost pointing the way to various parts of the hospital, but there was no mention of an Adolescent Unit. I turned right and walked round until I came in sight of a new-looking building which I thought might be the Adolescent Unit, since our Adolescent Unit was a new building and, since they were a new idea, Adolescent Units were likely to be new, anyhow.

As I saw the lights of London skyscrapers in the distance, I thought, "This is a beautiful place!"

I examined the building and, as I saw some people playing table tennis who looked as if they were in their twenties, I decided that this was the Sports Centre, which had been signposted in that direction.

I wandered back to the seat and sat down and looked around me for about ten minutes.

Then I continued my pilgrimage.

I carried on walking round the hospital. I came to a sort of forecourt. In the darkness, it looked like a lake with overhanging trees from a distance.

As I wandered farther up into a space in the centre of the hospital, I saw a modern building with lights on in which people, young people were sitting and eating at the far end of a long dining room. I couldn't make out how young they were.

On the wall outside the building was a notice which said, "STAFF CANTEEN". But it looked as if there were two canteens, one being at the end from which I was looking. However, I came to the conclusion that the whole building was the staff canteen and not an Adolescent Unit with the staff canteen at one end.

I came back and walked across the field where they played football. I passed down the street and waved to the headmaster. I walked in and had a look at the inkwells, and came down the corridor where we shifted the piano back from the Scripture Union, into the classroom where the meetings were held. The teacher was there. She walked through the door in the glass partition to the other classroom. I walked out to the playground, through the space in the wall to the square where we played.

This was in the year before the summer I was put in hospital, after which I had a dream in which I was back at the same school doing all right.

I came out of the school and along the road to where I went for a walk quietly to the vague noise of traffic in the night, and gazed across backyards to the former headmaster's house on the hill, which lay across the road from our own.

I felt that I would like to be a patient in the hospital and be with adolescents.

I felt that I wanted to draw a picture of them, some naked, some half-dressed.

October – December 1974

Lightning Source UK Ltd.
Milton Keynes UK
UKOW04f2034170913

217403UK00001B/13/P